IN SEARCH OF SELF

Cowley Publications is a work of the Society of St. John the Evangelist, a religious community for men in the Episcopal Church. The books we publish are a significant part of our ministry, together with the work of preaching, spiritual direction, and hospitality. Our aim is to provide books that will enrich their readers' religious experience and challenge it with fresh approaches to religious concerns.

In Search of Self
Life, Death and Walker Percy

Jerome Taylor

Published in the United States of America
by Cowley Publications

Grateful acknowledgment is made to Farrar, Straus & Giroux, Inc. for permission to quote from the following works by Walker Percy: *The Last
Gentleman*, copyright © 1966 by Walker Percy; *Love in the Ruins*,
copyright © 1971 by Walker Percy; *The Message in the Bottle*, copyright ©
1954, 1956, 1957, 1958, 1959, 1961, 1967, 1972, 1975 by Walker Percy;
Lancelot, copyright © 1977 by Walker Percy; *The Second Coming*,
copyright © 1980 by Walker Percy.

Søren Kierkegaard, *Either/Or*, trans. David F. Swenson and Lillian Marvin
Swenson. Copyright 1944, © 1972 by Howard A. Johnson and published by
Princeton University Press. Excerpts reprinted by permission of Princeton
University Press.

Library of Congress Cataloging-in-Publication Data

Taylor, L. Jerome.
    In search of self, life, death, and Walker Percy.

    Bibliography: p.
    1. Percy, Walker, 1916-   --Characters.
2. Percy, Walker, 1916-   --Philosophy.
3. Kierkegaard, Soren, 1813-1855--Influence.
4. Self (Philosophy) in literature.   I. Title.
PS3566.E6912Z84 1986   813'.54   86-4194
ISBN 0-936384-32-8 (pbk.)

COWLEY PUBLICATIONS
980 MEMORIAL DRIVE
CAMBRIDGE, MA 02138

FOR POLLY

Contents

Chapter 1

In Search of Self

One needs only to be alive, to look around and think about things a little to be aware that all is not well in the Western world. And from what we hear of the East, the Middle East, or even South of the Border, there is no reason to think things are much better in those places either. Much is written about what is wrong, much of it no doubt true and much of it perhaps simply wasted effort. This book is an attempt to convey the insights and the urgings of two men, one of nineteenth century Denmark and the other of our own time and place, about the wrongness of our world. The former is widely acknowledged to have had hold of something that can make all the difference for us if we let ourselves see and act upon it. He is Søren Kierkegaard, Danish philosopher, poet, and ardent advocate of the individual human person. The novelist of our own era who I believe embodies Kierkegaard's philosophy and whose works may open our eyes to ourselves, is Walker Percy.

Among philosophers today Kierkegaard is accorded the title "father of modern existentialism." Existentialism is the rather broad movement of thought, ranging from atheistic to Christian, that insists that the important concern is the existing person as over against any speculative intellectual system. Existentialism emphasizes that the existing person's central task in life is to acquire his or her own selfhood through personal choice and action. Kierkegaard was acutely sensitive to the ways in which our scientific age tends to subvert us from making the "inner movements" that lead to becoming a self in the real sense. Mass communication, for example, tends to pull each person into thinking like all the rest instead of seeing and acting independently. This is only a modern intensification of the ageless human tendency to conform to the expectations and fashions of the crowd in order to feel secure.

In any case, philosophy today acknowledges that Kierkegaard's awareness of growing danger, his passion for individual integrity and freedom, made him the first modern philosopher-theologian to come to grips with these very twentieth century facts of life. He was intuitively aware of the threat of technology, which was only beginning to take form in his day. The various kinds of depersonalizations we experience daily—resulting from the mere bigness of business, government, mass media, and the like—are taking their toll and making the central human task of self-becoming more problematic than ever. Kierkegaard's influence on contemporary life and thought continues to be immense and is reflected in the works of Jean Paul Sartre, Albert Camus, and Martin Heidegger, as well as in modern psychological theory and practice. He was the determinative influence on perhaps the two most important Christian theologians of the twentieth century: Rudolph Bultmann and Karl Barth.

Kierkegaard is the guiding light of another of our own era, the novelist Walker Percy who, like Kierkegaard, speaks with wry sarcasm and humor to our self-imposed plight and attempts through indirection to stir us out of it. Percy came to his profession after suffering a serious illness and other personal losses as a young man. During this period he was deeply affected by the works of Kierkegaard, whose perception of the human he shares. He is concerned, as was the Danish philosopher, about what he sees happening to people today; he also sees essentially the same cure and is full of the delightful, subtly bizarre humor that so frequently cropped up in Kierkegaard. Percy conveys the curative insights of his mentor through the lives of the characters in his stories. The hero or protagonist in each case is a person who makes the movement from a kind of death-in-life to a finding of himself such that "he who was dead is alive again."

The death-in-life that Kierkegaard in his day and Percy in ours are so concerned about is widely recognized. Pick up any popular magazine, and one finds recurring descriptions and explanations that attempt to deal with what is happening. The world, especially the Western world, has become markedly more depersonalized than it was even 130 years ago when Kierkegaard was writing. The old values are losing their grip on us, values that nourish and sustain the human, that bring out the human and affirm it. The soaring divorce rate is a telling indicator. Prevailing mores seem to make fidelity and care for the other person secondary to looking out for "number one." A "me generation" finds its bonding cement crumbling, and flippancy and thrill-seeking hide the great emptiness experienced in the loss of enduring relationships.

The shallowness of so many people today is reflected in the quality of television, movies, books, Broadway. How hard it is, for example, to find a dramatic production that deals with real life in the midst of cream-puff musicals and Neil Simon comedies. Yet these symptoms are also frightening. We are beginning more and more to ask, whom can we trust? In the past did we have to lock the car every time we got out of it? Were we apprehensive about walking out of our house at night? What is causing this violence and fear?

Near the end of Percy's latest novel an ancient but clear-eyed Episcopal priest, who has recently returned to his homeland, America, after fifty years as a missionary in the Philippines, expresses his sadness at what he finds:

> "How can we be the best dearest most generous people on earth and at the same time so unhappy? How harsh everyone is here! How restless! How impatient! How worried! How sarcastic! How unhappy! How hateful! How pleasure-loving! How lascivious! Above all, how selfish! Why is it that we have more than any other people, are more generous with what we have, and yet are so selfish and unhappy? Why do we think of nothing but our own pleasure? I cannot believe my eyes at what I see on television. It makes me blush with shame. Did you know that pleasure-seeking leads to cruelty? That is why more people beat their children. Children interfere with pleasure. Do you hate children? Why can't we be grateful for our great blessings and thank God?" As he gazed down at the desk he seemed to have

forgotten Will Barrett. His voice sank to a whisper. "Why is it that Americans who are the best dearest most generous people on earth are so unhappy?" He shook his head. "I don't——" (*SC*, 359).

It is no exaggeration to say that Percy is a modern-day seer who sees and tells what he sees in contemporary American life.

Seemingly minor and humorous symptoms are also held up by Percy as pointers to this serious condition. He bemoans the fact that whereas in times past on the golf course when he would ask his experienced black caddy what club he should use, he would get a human response—"That's a *spoon* shot."—now he extracts a numbered club from the back of an electric cart. Fads, in-words pick everybody up in their brief swirl and then something else comes along. Tennis lasts for a while, and then it's jogging that we are "into," training for the marathon. Allie, in *The Second Coming*, has just emerged from two years in a mental hospital, and she returns to the outside world with eyes that are fresh to see, as was the case with Rip Van Winkle. She observes that people hardly make declarative statements any more. It's too risky. They often speak only in phrases, heavily laced with "like" and "you know" and "really." Many attempts at statements are expressed as a kind of question, with the voice going up at the end. The strange new styles of living that she sees are indications that people have abandoned their "I," that they are afraid to live it and assert it. Where is the robust, personal subject, the one who knows what he wants, says it, and does it? Kierkegaard and Percy believe that we are in danger of becoming mass men and women; we hide in the herd for ease and safety. Pop psychology is obviously aware of the problem and is on the right track at least, even if one-sidedly and superficially, in calling us to assert ourselves.

All of these things Kierkegaard saw coming 140 years ago, and the symptoms have advanced apace since. Percy sees it all and groans. He sees it as his mission, as did Kierkegaard, to "wound us from behind," to wake us up, because we could sleep-walk in lock step to our death, never having lived. Percy says in *The Moviegoer* that the time is late, too late to be edifying in quite the same manner that Kierkegaard was, "if indeed ass kicking is properly distinguished from edification." (*M*, 237).

The problem, as Kierkegaard diagnosed it, lies in our failure to grapple with and undertake the central task of our lives. This task, laid on everyone, is that of "becoming an individual." Everything else—what one does for a living, where one lives, whom one marries, one's ethical choices—is secondary to this main task, even though these form the necessary context in which one engages, or fails to engage, in the task. What did Kierkegaard mean by the term, becoming an individual? He meant standing out from the crowd, seeing with one's eyes and acting in accordance with one's inner desires, promptings, and goals. Most of us, most of the time, Kierkegaard said, are not our own persons but are led around and dance to the tune of all kinds of external events, ideas, fashions, and the like. We do what we see other people doing. We "aim to please." We get married because it's the thing to do; we stay in the same rut all our lives in order not to risk too much. This is what Kierkegaard called the aesthetic mode of existence: being determined by that which is outside ourselves, and therefore not being free. The external determinant of sex, for example, is an especially powerful lure that can take us away from our real, acting, deciding selves. Envision a young man consumed with the highly enjoyable passion of pursuing women. Is he in charge of his life or is he not instead being pulled around by the nose? All of this is very pleasant, but as long as his life is determined by external factors—the opposite sex, the admiration of his peers, or even the thirst for great learning—he is not really free and has not yet begun to live his own life.

This kind of chasing after external lures, Kierkegaard insists, is at bottom a doomed effort to evade the anxiety inherent in the human condition. Human anxiety, he says, stems from the fact that we are not simply animal creatures; we are also composed of an essential component of the infinite. We are not just flesh; we are also spirit. We are urged and impelled from somewhere inside ourselves to do and go beyond where we are; and as long as we evade this urging through pursuing external diversions of the moment, a gnawing anxiety works in us, a feeling of self-betrayal and of guilt. Ever faster running after immediate gratification may cover up the anxiety for a time, but the only way to get on to selfhood is to break away from this narcotic, face around, and stay in the "despair," as Kierkegaard calls it, until we are finally enabled to "leap" into a second mode of existence. This new mode will be what he calls "the ethical stage," where instead of running around diverting ourselves we begin on the more serious life-style of taking responsibility for ourselves and others. We begin to act in responsible ways—caring for others and for our own welfare, doing what needs to be done, getting a job to feed and clothe the baby, etc.

Kierkegaard sees the movement to selfhood as taking place through stages. In the aesthetic stage one has not yet started to exist as an individual. A person may stay in this stage all of his or her life if he or she continues to successfully find ways to divert from the inner despair, the sense of failure at being stuck at this way-station.

In its turn, however, the ethical stage is not a permanent stage either, simply because human beings are not constituted with adequate power to accomplish the infinite demands of the ethical. We have neither sufficient vision, endurance, nor inclination to do what needs to be done for our own best interests. Thus, sooner or later we come up against failure. As Kierkegaard puts it, the ethical stage, like the aesthetic, finally "comes to grief on time"; sooner or later one's weakness trips him up. When the ethical striving toward victory finally crumbles under foot, the individual must either fall into oblivion or make another leap; this time, of necessity, into help from the Beyond. One thus moves, not by a gradual process nor by simple resolution of the will, but, nevertheless, by definite inner movements into the "religious mode of existence."

If one is to come alive, one must choose and perform the inner actions necessary to move from one stage to the next toward increasing selfhood. One is free to hang on to the pleasurable diversions of the aesthetic stage if one so chooses; but if one is willing to stop running in this way from the self and turn and experience the *angst* of simply standing there unprotected, the individual, says Kierkegaard, "gains possession of himself." The one injunction that Kierkegaard urges upon the ever-running aesthete is, "Choose despair." That is, stop running away from yourself. You will then begin to become a self, to move out from the crowd and to live by your own lights. This is the essential movement from death into life and constitutes the beginning of a "God-relationship." The further movement into the religious mode *per se*, however, is the only viable step when one has, through bitter experience, discovered the limits of an individual's power to live in the ethical. It is not a movement that can be coolly planned or willed; as such it will fail. It is a possibility that is thrust upon the person when he or she has attained a certain point in life. Many times this opportunity presents itself, and many times the movement must be repeated because selfhood must be continually reacquired.

The way to selfhood, or faith, was Kierkegaard's consuming interest. Johannes *de silentio*, Kierkegaard's pseudonymous author of *Fear and Trembling*, says:

> But if I knew where there was such a knight of faith, I would make a pilgrimage to him on foot, for this prodigy interests me absolutely. I would not let him go for an instant, every moment I would watch to see how he managed to make the movements. I would regard myself as secured for life, and would divide my time between looking at him and practicing the exercises myself, and thus would spend all my time admiring him (*FT*, 49).

It is necessary to stress that in both Kierkegaard's and Percy's views, the essential element in the whole process of self-becoming is what might be called "miracle." Throughout the process there is that working which is beyond the planning and the power of the person. Percy depicts his protagonists at the opening of each novel as, in one way or another, living on the brink. In *The Second Coming* Will Barrett is flirting dangerously with suicide, drawn to it almost irresistibly. Percy refers occasionally to Kierkegaard's wry remark about the young man who had it made in every aspect of his life, with the sole exception of having trouble finding a way to live from one ordinary moment to the next on a Wednesday afternoon. Percy states it even more chillingly: "But the hero of the post-modern novel is a man who has forgotten his bad memories and conquered his present ills and who finds himself in the victorious secular city. His only problem now is to keep from blowing his brains out" (*MB*, 112). The movement out of the deathly aesthetic mode to the ethico-religious is *enabled* by something beyond the protagonist's own will power. He must assent and make the inner movement, and in this act he is enabled. One makes the choice to "hang in there," but the breakthrough comes from beyond. "Suddenly the thunderstorm breaks," as Kierkegaard puts it in describing the breakthrough into the religious stage.

We must observe a cautionary note here, however, lest we fall into an overly neat classification of the complexities of human existence. A person is an unstable being and often slips back from a more advanced stage to a lesser one—from the religious to the ethical and from both to the aesthetic. Kierkegaard was well aware of this basic problem.

> It requires a very different talent for brevity to describe the victory of faith in half an hour [in the pulpit] than to describe what an ordinary man fills out the day with in the living room. . . . But what all is not required to present a human being as he is in daily life! If only language does not embarrass one by revealing itself as insufficient, because it is so abstract in comparison with existing, in the sense which this has in reality (*CUP*, 415).

Kierkegaard did not intend to give the impression that the "stages" are stations through which a person simply progresses, leaving one behind as he or she arrives at the next. He was trying to show three ways of existing which are mutually exclusive when regarded as the determining focus of a person's life but which tend to overlap into the adjacent mode, both up and down the line. For example, he makes the point that "the aesthetic is not abolished but is merely dethroned" when one makes the decisive movement from the aesthetic to the ethico-religious stage. Furthermore, any study of the human must acknowledge that one cannot tell what is going on inside another person; as Kierkegaard says, one cannot tell a "knight of faith" merely by looking at him. A true knight will usually look from the outside like any happy, mature, perhaps even successful person. This is so because the movements, the choices, the sacrifice of natural instincts that enable one to respond to the eternal are inner movements. "The true form of the comic is that the infinite may move within a man, and no one, be able to discover it through anything appearing outwardly" (CUP, 84).

Kierkegaard believed that talking about movement to selfhood in an abstract or general way is ineffective in view of the particularities of human existence. The only valid medium, he felt, is that of concrete examples, so he created what he called his "marionette theater" of fictional persons. What follows, in part, are key representatives from his marionette theater, presented side by side with contemporary characters from Percy's novels to help us see what kinds of choices may lead to selfhood.

The essential purpose of this study is to show one perceptive modern novelist's view of what new and recovered life is like, and of what is required of the person if he or she would achieve it. What Percy describes as the final position of his protagonists is certainly what Kierkegaard would have called religious faith or "selfhood before God," even though Percy's characters seem not necessarily to have conscious awareness of God. Through their search and their choices, they have moved into new relationships to their own selves and to life, which is essentially the same as the religious attitude of faith. They know who they are, and they know they are not the center of their own existence but rather are vitally related to something beyond themselves. In each case, as Percy sees it, this something, which is truly the wellspring of life for them, is mediated through the friendship and love of a person. The miracle of grace in the movement to this secular style of faith is no less real than it is in the more explicitly God-conscious style that seems to be in decline today. Percy's protagonists are led on a journey, and the final breakthrough to selfhood seems clearly to come as a gift from beyond themselves. Percy's great contribution is to suggest to modern persons who have given up on God and faith that new possibilities may even now be overtaking them.

Chapter 2

Seduction and Despair

If it is true, as our subjects insist, that one is "dead, dead, dead," to use Percy's phrase, who has not broken out of what Kierkegaard calls the aesthetic mode, then it would seem of first importance to see more specifically what constitutes living in this limited way. In this chapter, I will attempt to sketch what Kierkegaard's genius led him to see as this deadly trap and will follow in the next with Percy's way of seeing the same basic phenomenon.

As indicated, Kierkegaard claims that existence in the aesthetic mode is essentially non-existence, while even a beginning existence in the ethico-religious is the start of concrete selfhood. It may help to know that, by definition, a person seriously struggling with this question is already out of the aesthetic mode, because in the aesthetic mode one does not reflect on one's life. When one's existence is in the aesthetic mode, he or she is essentially a passive responder to the many lures, attractions, and diversions that life offers. Everyone, of course, can be diverted by the desires of the moment to some extent. The difference between this and living in the aesthetic mode, however, has to do with whether one is determined by that which is outside himself or whether one tends more to see and act on his own. In the latter case, one is a free, acting individual; in the former, one is a mere floater, a parasite on the flux of time and events.

The dominating characteristic of the aesthetic stage, says Kierkegaard, is enjoyment. An actor whose life is moved primarily by desire for the approval of an audience exists in the aesthetic stage. So also does the ambitious corporate executive whose overriding concern is advancement, with its various perquisites of prestige, money, and power. The aesthetic stage even includes the person whose absorbing appetite is for greater and greater knowledge or for developing a talent. A person who lives mainly for the next party, the weekend, or for getting out in his boat is certainly in this mode. The bumper sticker "I'd rather be sailing" is indicative of where, if Kierkegaard's and Percy's insights are accurate, vast numbers of our age may live—in the aesthetic mode of existence.

DON JUAN

It may not be easy for the twentieth-century reader to grasp the seemingly abstract notion of existing in a certain mode, especially when it is claimed to have such decisive consequences. For this reason Kierkegaard used representative individuals to embody his ideas. The most remarkable of these was the legendary medieval character, Don Juan. Knowing that his essential characteristic was that he was completely captured by the seductive lure of the opposite sex should immediately help us to see what Kierkegaard is talking about. Don Juan's very life lay in the pursuit and conquest of women. He was passionately in love with each of these in the brief moment of his involvement with her, but none of them meant anything to him as can be seen by the fact that he could never remember any of them and thus had to keep a list! Kierkegaard tells us that Don Juan seduced 1003 young ladies "in Spain alone"!

But Don Juan is not a humorous figure. He is a powerful and tragic figure and exerts a seductive influence on those around him. His power is in his passion and his thirst for fulfillment. "The reaction to this gigantic passion beautifies and develops the one desired, who flushes in enhanced beauty by its reflection" (*E/OI, 98*).

When a person's life is determined by enjoyment, he or she

experiences life only in the moment. "And this, again," says Judge William of *Either/Or*, "is the most adequate expression for aesthetic existence: it is in the moment" (*E/OII, 234*). In this way of living one tends to go, at each moment, in whatever direction may be found the greatest level of gratification. A sense of responsibility for the past or future is not a significant element in this consciousness.

By contrast, a person living in the ethical mode of existence assumes responsibilities which require him or her to make difficult choices and to act. Time then becomes an essential factor. The ethicist sees what he must do in the future and does it; he looks back upon what he has done in the past and bears responsibility for it. Judge William, Kierkegaard's fictional ethicist, and Don Juan live in sharp contrast to each other in this regard. Don Juan, living for the moment of pleasure with his series of 1003 damsels, does not experience continuity with himself through time; his life is lived for the moment. Judge William, on the other hand, is married to one woman for life. Memory, promises, fidelity, and growth in relationship, which are essential to a lifelong commitment, obviously have time as a basic ingredient.

To live for the moment of gratification by external means is to be determined by fate. Kierkegaard says, "Fortune, misfortune, fate, immediate enthusiasm, despair—these are the categories at the disposal of an aesthetic view of life" (*CUP, 388*). The aesthete is happy and contented as long as good fortune continues. When misfortune comes, however, he is cast into despair but assumes that it will soon pass away because it is a foreign element. The fact that a person is able to stay in the aesthetic mode only as long as good fortune continues accounts for the aesthete's mood of exuberance.

The true and underlying condition of the aesthete, however —that from which in all his activity he is trying to escape—is despair. Of the aesthetic mode, Kierkegaard asserts:

> Melancholy is its essential character, and this so deep, that though autopathic it deceptively occupies itself with the sufferings of others, and for the rest deceives by concealing itself under the cloak of pleasure, rationality, demoralization (*CUP, 226*).

A reason for the despair in the aesthetic mode of living, says Kierkegaard, is that:

> His life view thus hinges upon a condition which is not in his power ... But every life view which hinges upon a condition outside itself is despair ... since it always is despair to have one's life dependent upon that which may pass away (E/OII, 240).

As previously indicated, however, the reason for the despair of the aesthete goes deeper and is due to his repression of his own self, of that element of himself which is part of the eternal.

A primary characteristic of the aesthetic manner of living is the seductive spell that it tends to cast. Kierkegaard in his later years said that one of the central concerns in his work had been to "denounce the magical charms of aesthetics"; but, noting his scant results, he observes that "privately, with secret passion, they love that magic" (PV, 29). In order to escape the void that is experienced when one refuses relationship to one's own self, a person seeks the narcotic of forgetfulness by following the escape of the moment. In so doing he finds himself bound in a spell and seduced from life.

> For the idea of there being peace and safety, and men's assurance about it, is like a spell which readily deceives with its powerful stupefaction, and the entire strength of the soul is needed to wrest oneself free from this delusion (EDI, 213).

As he becomes aware of his despair, Kierkegaard concludes here, the person "vainly [seeks] a hiding place among the throngs of men." He speaks repeatedly of "the crowd" and how conformity to its opinions can lure a person away from selfhood (PV, 112). The aesthete thus lives an "imagination existence" in self-deception and concealment. He has yet to "gain a history" and in so doing finally be on the way to becoming a self (CUP, 226-7).

What we see in Don Juan, then, is the personification of exuberance of life, its joy and its perfect confidence in victory. But always underlying this is the despair. His sensuous desire so powerfully connects him with the woman with whom he is momentarily involved that he is incapable of any reflection which could lead him to a more responsible manner of life. The energy and force of his desire is the source of his power over others (*E/O* I, 98).

An important point to note in Don Juan is that the object of his desire is not a particular woman but sensuousness itself. He is not even a seducer in the true sense of the word because "to be a seducer requires a certain amount of reflection and consciousness." If Don Juan had this, he would already have broken the spell of immediacy in which he is lost. The fact that he does not love a particular woman helps to explain why he is continually in the moment and hurrying to the next. It is the new that he desires along with the sensuous, and a particular woman loses the interest of novelty through the passage of time.

> He desires sensuously, he seduces with the demonic power of sensuousness, he seduces everyone. Speech, dialogue are not for him, for then he would be at once a reflective individual. Thus he does not have a stable existence at all, but he hurries in a perpetual vanishing, precisely like music, about which it is true that it is over as soon as it has ceased to sound, and only comes into being when it again sounds (*E/O* I, 101).

To live in sensuous immediacy is to live a surface life of happiness and confident exuberance. "Most men," says Kierkegaard, "live a long time in aesthetic immediacy or spontaneity . . . all their many happy years of immediacy tend toward spiritual retardation" (*JH* II, 1123).

The power of vital natural forces keeps the aesthetic mode of existence alive. The poet in Kierkegaard, speaking in the voice of the aesthete, can help one feel the strong attraction of this way of life.

> It is powerful as the thought of a god, moving as a world's life, trembling in its earnestness, quivering in its passion, crushing in its terrible wrath, inspiring in its joy of life; it is faithful in its judgement, strident in its lust, it is deliberately solemn in its imposing dignity, it is stirring, flaming, dancing in its joy (*E/O* I, 126).

Many facets of life lived in pursuit of a superficial fulfillment come out in the above, and one can hardly wonder at the seductive power of it. However, the *angst* from which this way is trying to escape is ever present; and when in time one's luck runs out or one's vital powers fade, the occasion may be providential in making possible the leap to selfhood.

Don Juan is only the most striking of the examples that Kierkegaard gives of the aesthetic mode, and his exaggerated life should not be allowed to mislead us. Aesthetic pursuit takes place in more familiar forms, and Kierkegaard provides many examples. "This is the case," he says, "with every view of life where wealth, glory, high station, etc. are accounted life's task and content." He goes on to cite such activities as devoting one's life to developing a talent, preservation and enhancement of one's health or beauty, the lust for fishing, hunting, or keeping horses, etc. (*E/O* II, 187, 188).

FAUST

There is another important way of avoiding being a self that Kierkegaard describes as higher or a step beyond this way, and that is what he sometimes describes as a "poet existence." As Percy sees it, this way of avoiding being one's own self is widespread and pernicious today but difficult to spot. Broadly speaking, the novelist would say, it is a matter of having one's life dominated by external ideas and images. In our own age the determinative images are those proclaimed by science. Science deals in universals and asserts universal hypotheses and laws as being the truth about individual concrete phenomena. We tend to fall into attitudes and see the general law as more real than the concrete events in which we exist. For example, we may give precedence to the certified opinion of the experts over our own particular vision and judgment. Thus, again, we lose ourselves; this time not to the sensuous immediacy of the warm flesh of one of Don Juan's ladies but to the abstract idea. It is quite a different style than that of Don Juan, but it shares the essential feature of aesthetic existence in that the person's life is determined by that which is outside the self. Kierkegaard used the figure of Faust to present certain characteristics of this form of aestheticism. Faust's life was given to the pursuit of abstract truth. It is symbolic that he sold his soul to the Devil in order to attain intellectual truth, because his pursuit is away from persons and toward a solitary hell. He is not a sovereign being, seeing and acting in the world, but only another passive consumer.

Faust is said by Kierkegaard to be "demonic," meaning that he is captured by an alien spirit. Percy believes that modern man is captured by controlling ideas certified by the experts. To that extent we are like Faust, captured by and lost to a demon. Faust must acquire more and more knowledge but does not let that knowledge have any affect on what he does. We might say his life is not in gear; his motor is racing at high speed, but in neutral. Since he can never be sure that he is finding the essential truth he is looking for, he becomes increasingly doubtful—doubtful of what he has found already and of the possibility of finding any final answer. Instead of facing up to his doubt and risking action, he prefers to divert himself with "thought experiments."

Kierkegaard portrays Faust as being always in a hurry, "constantly hovering above himself." His sad state is expressed in the ironic words of the "Diapsalmata":

> Generally speaking, I lack the patience to live. I cannot see the grass grow, but since I cannot, I do not care to look at it at all. My views are the fleeting observations of a "traveling scholastic," rushing through life in greatest haste. People say that the good Lord fills the stomach before the eyes; I have not noticed it; my eyes are sated and weary of everything, and yet I hunger (E/O I, 24).

Kierkegaard observes that Faust wants to become "sheer spirit." He is alone, cut off from any real human relationships and their attendant responsibilities because he is constantly abstracting from them into the realm of his ideas. The young man of "in Vino Veritas" removes himself from what could begin his return to life in the ordinary world as he says, "I will not love anybody before I have fathomed the thought of love, and that I am not able to do; on the contrary, I have reached the conclusion that love is comic" (*SLW*, 52). "Woe to him who is thus solitary," says Judge William of *Either/Or*, "he is deserted by the whole of existence." To be pulled into the seductive atmosphere of abstract ideas is to be cut off from people and the concrete life supports they give. Faust's means of escape from the claims of others is essentially the same as that of Don Juan: ". . . that combination of imagination and intelligence where the factor of the will is lacking is really sensuality" (*JD*, 448). Kierkegaard knew of what he spoke because this was his own tendency in his youth.

In his isolation Faust tries to find his way back to the solid world of the human by means of the sensuous. Mephistopheles shows him Margaret in a mirror, and Faust seeks solace in her.

> His doubting soul finds nothing in which it can rest, and now he reaches after love, not because he believes in it, but because it has a present element in which there is rest for a moment, and a striving which distracts and diverts his attention from the nothingness of doubt . . .

> As the shades of the underworld, when they get hold of a living being, sucked his blood, and lived as long as this blood warmed and nourished them, so Faust seeks an immediate life by which he can be renewed and strengthened. And where can this be found better than in a young woman, and how can he absorb it more perfectly than in the embrace of love (*E/O* I, 204–205)?

What a pathetic creature then is Faust, the one who gives up all for the lure of knowledge. He is a mere "shade," a ghost. Because he has tried to escape from life into the realm of ideas, his sick soul is languishing for "a young heart's first green shoots." What he longs for is "the pure, rich, untroubled, immediate happiness of a woman's soul," but he desires it sensuously to fill his need and not as a real relationship, again like Don Juan. It is her "innocent simplicity" based on an immediate faith which he needs. He must build her faith in order to enjoy it, and to do this he must stay with Margaret instead of moving on as Don Juan does. He must concentrate on this one woman and is careful not to let her faith be destroyed by seeing his doubt. In the process her faith is transferred to him, to his apparent superiority and power. This is no concern to him as long as his needs are being filled. It is in this light that the full extent of his demonic nature appears as kin to the bloodsucking "shade of the underworld" which destroys its victim in order temporarily to maintain its own life. Faust knows that his sustenance from Margaret is only transient; "he does not believe in it any more than he believes in anything else." He knows, however, that it at least exists for the moment, and this is the only kind of existence that there is in the aesthetic mode.

In summary, then, the fundamental characteristic of one living in aesthetic immediacy is that of not having begun the task of acquiring his or her own self. When an individual simply responds to elements external to the self, he or she has not begun to exercise selfhood. The person must make a break with such immediacy in order to begin to live on his or her own. Exhortations to do this will not work because the aesthete does not live in a modality that can respond to them. Only the process of life can provide the way, and it does so by intensifying despair: that is, when despair intensifies, one may finally act.

> The ethicist had with the passion of the infinite in the moment of despair chosen himself out of the fearful plight of having his self, his life, his reality in aesthetic dreams, in melancholy, in concealment (*CUP*, 231).

We shall consider the break with aesthetics in a subsequent chapter. First, however, let us consider Walker Percy's distinctive contributions to our understanding of the aesthetic mode.

Chapter 3

Beasts and Angels

Walker Percy's understanding of the fundamental predicament of our human condition and the way to overcome it can best be understood if we take up the characters in his novels. Their lives embody what Kierkegaard saw as the three stages of existence, but his focus is on the aesthetic and the religious. Percy's indebtedness to Kierkegaard is clear. He has referred to the latter as "the greatest philosoper of the modern age," the one who "saw it most clearly" among all the other existentialist figures (*GR*, 321). This does not mean that as a novelist portraying persons in actual existence he is bound to any abstractly articulated philosophical position. He admits, however, to having been influenced by other existentialists in addition to Kierkegaard, including Heidegger, Marcel, Sartre, and Camus, and by philosophers concerned with symbolism and language, particularly Susanne Langer and Noam Chomsky.

Before looking at the fictional characters themselves, it may be helpful to have an overview of the basic ways in which Percy sees people slipping off into aesthetic evasions of life. For this, we shall deal primarily with his published essays in order to trace some of his major themes.

Percy's insights regarding persons, how they fail and how they may be set aright, are rooted in his understanding of our unique nature among the rest of the animal kingdom. He describes himself as among those novelists who have "an explicit and ultimate concern with the nature of man and the nature of reality where man finds himself" (*MB*, 102). Nowhere in his writings does he describe and systematically analyze man's nature. His views clearly emerge, however, both in his fiction and his essays.

The essence of Percy's position is suggested in the following excerpt from an essay he wrote on contemporary psychiatric practice:

> The issue is simply this: is psychiatry a biological science in which man is treated as an organism with instinctive drives and needs not utterly or qualitatively different from those of other organisms? Or is psychiatry a humanistic discipline which must take account of man as possessing a unique destiny by which he is oriented in a wholly different direction (*Amer*, 391)?

His own view is clearly the latter. He goes on to note the silence of American psychiatry on "the great themes which have engaged the existentialist critics of modern society from Søren Kierkegaard to Gabriel Marcel," and says that this silence is "because, given its basic concept of man, it is *unable* to take account of the predicament of modern man (Ibid., 392)." He observes that the scientist who regards persons as organisms shaped entirely by natural causes is really engaging in a double standard, one for his data and another for himself. How else, he asks, can Freud's theory of the interaction of forces as the explanation for human behavior be made to jibe with Freud's own passionate and lifelong quest for truth?

Percy values science highly, is scientifically trained as a physician, and is himself influenced by its methods and its questions, which are central to his own work. However, he has acknowledged that Kierkegaard helped him to see the shortcomings of science. He cites Kierkegaard's wry statement that "Hegel told everything about the world except one thing: what it is to be a man and to live and die" (*Shen*, 4).

Percy's position against the "objective-biological" concept of human life centers around his assumption that there are important areas of human need and experience which are not amenable to the biological approach. He cites particularly the need for or experience of "relatedness" and "transcendence." He states:

> We all know perfectly well that the man who lives out his life as a consumer, a sexual partner, an "other-directed" executive; who avoids boredom and anxiety by consuming tons of newsprint, miles of movie film, years of TV time; that such a man has somehow betrayed his destiny as a human being (*Amer*, 415).

The factor of "transcendence," of which the biological understanding of humanity cannot take account, is one, Percy says, that all existentialists agree upon in one form or another, from Gabriel Marcel's idea of man's "true motion toward God" to Jean Paul Sartre's "absurd striving, the 'useless passion.'" "Even the atheistic existentialists," says Percy, "would be candid enough to admit man's incurable God-directedness."

What, then, does this tell us about the actual nature of human beings in Percy's view? He employs two related metaphors to describe this nature: Gabriel Marcel's "wayfarer" and his own, "castaway" (*MB*, 119). Both of these images convey his idea of human nature as a synthesis of organism and spirit. He describes man "as by his very nature an exile and a wanderer" whose primary need is that of "recovering himself as neither angel nor organism but as a wayfaring creature somewhere between." His language here is strikingly similar to that used by Kierkegaard in a similar context and points up the essential agreement of their views. Kierkegaard put it this way:

> If a man were a beast or an angel, he would not be able to be in dread. Since he is a synthesis he can be in dread, and the greater the dread, the greater the man (*CD*, 139).

The nature of the human as seen by Percy, then, is essentially that of a synthesis, too, and this he sees as the root of our problem.

> Yet even so all is not well with him. Something is wrong. For with all the knowledge he achieves, all his art and philosophy, all the island news he pays attention to, something is missing. What is it? He does not know. He might say that he was homesick except that the island is his home and he has spent his life making himself at home there . . .
>
> But how does he know he is sick, let alone homesick? He may not know. He may live and die as an islander at home on his island. But if he does know, he knows for the simple reason that in his heart of hearts he can never forget who he is: that he is a stranger, a castaway, who despite a life time of striving to be at home on the island is as homeless now as he was the first day he found himself cast up on the beach (*MB*, 143).

Our in-between state is one of pain and one that we constantly tend to evade. It is a state that is not at home in the purely finite world and is, says Percy, like finding oneself on an island as a castaway who has lost his memory in the shipwreck and does not know where he came from or who he is (*MB*, 119). Kierkegaard expresses this same self-awareness in terms of what he calls the "moment of eternity" within oneself. As Kierkegaard scholar Peter Rohde put it, "however slowly and dreamlike this moment of eternity manifests itself within him, it is there, and this dreaming consciousness fosters *angst*" (*SK*, 161). It is the awareness of possibility and freedom that is both man's joy and his burden. When he avoids the call of spirit, the awareness of which comes at certain moments of clarity, he fails himself. When he thus refuses to choose or act he remains in despair, regardless of whether he feels this or not.

The awareness of eternity calling one to freedom and action is the basis of another aspect of the human condition which Percy calls our "unformulability." Everything around us can be formulated by a symbol. By the human act of symbolizing we are related to our environment. There is, however, says Percy "one tremendous exception":

> The one thing in the world which by its very nature is not susceptible of a stable symbolic transformation is *myself*! I, who symbolize the world in order to know it, am destined to remain forever unknown to myself (*MB*, 283).

Thus one's self must remain unformulable, and Percy borrows Marcel's phrase—"the aching wound of self"—to describe it (*PPR*, 527–30). He shares with other existentialists the view that the state of man is radically ambiguous, indeterminate, and in opposition to itself. Along with Kierkegaard he sees that the contradictions of life are primarily within the human person and not in external circumstances. He acknowledges that his own understanding of man's natue is explicitly the Christian one:

> As it happens, I speak in a Christian context. That is to say, I do not conceive it my vocation to preach the Christian faith in a novel, but as it happens, my world view is informed by a certain belief about man's nature and destiny which cannot fail to be central to any novel I write (*MB*, 111).

If our nature is the painful one of being both animal and spirit, how can we cope with it? This is Percy's central concern as he sees so many evading their life-task of becoming a self. "To be a castaway is to be in a grave predicament and this is not a happy state of affairs. But it is very much happier than being a castaway and pretending one is not. This is despair" (*MB*, 144). How, then, do we cope with this uncomfortable middle state? Unfortunately we too often do so, say Kierkegaard and Percy, by slipping away from the pain either by pretending we are beasts, following all the lures of appetite and ignoring the urgings of spirit, or by moving in the other direction to the realm of abstraction. The first is Don Juan, the second is Faust. In Percy's words "mankind is presently divided into two classes: the consumer, long since anesthetized and lost to himself in the rounds of consumership, and the 'stranded' objectified consciousness, a ghost of a man who wanders the earth like Ishmael" (*MB*, 115). It is by our own choice that we move toward one or the other of "this monstrous bifurcation . . . into angelic or beastly components." We are therefore responsible for the despair in which we find ourselves, guilty of betrayal of the human task. Percy thus clearly agrees with Kierkegaard's judgment that "despair is sin" (*SD*, 210).

24

Beastism

Percy sees two basic ways in which persons evade life within the first of these two opposite movements—that is, the one that adapts non-reflectively to the environment. These two ways are the "consumption of goods" and the "assumption of identities." In his essay "Symbol as Hermeneutic," Percy writes:

> In the "passive unauthentic self which has fallen prey to things," new things enter into the zone of the nought and are devoured. There is a real consumption of goods. A new product, an automobile, resplendent in its autonomous form . . . is loved for the sake of its form. . . . If I can have that car my life will be different, for my nothingness will be informed by the having of it. But possession turns out to be a gradual neutralization. Once it enters the zone of my nought, the car is emptied out, and instead of informing me, only participates in my nothingness. There is a dynamic quest for resplendent forms—in two separate moments: the assumption of identities (impersonation) and the consumption of goods (in order to be informed by them) (MB, 284).

The "consumer of goods" is "tranquilized in his never-ending consumption of goods, services, entertainment and human intercourse" (Amer, 392). He adapts to his finite environment in this way. The "impersonator," on the other hand, loses himself by pretending to be that which he thinks is acceptable. He pretends to be someone else or conforms to the crowd. He thus finds himself in what Kierkegaard calls "the despair of not willing to be himself" (SD, 182). The self will then, as Percy says, "fall prey to miserable unauthentic transformations" (MB, 284).

There are many variations on our ways of escaping the pain of selfhood by grasping after things in our environment. One of these is what both Kierkegaard and Percy call "rotation." Rotation, says Percy, "is the quest for the new as the new, the reposing of all hope in what may lie around the bend" (MB, 86). Kierkegaard, in his ironic/humorous vein, describes it this way:

> Rotation . . . depends on change in its boundless infinity, its extensive dimension, so to speak . . . One tires of living in the

country, and moves to the city; one tires of one's native land, and travels abroad; one is *europamüde*, and goes to America, and so on; finally one indulges in a sentimental hope of endless journeyings from star to star. Or the movement is different but still extensive. One tires of porcelain dishes and eats on silver; one tires of silver and turns to gold; one burns half of Rome to get an idea of the burning of Troy. This method defeats itself; it is plain endlessness (*E/O* I, 287-8).

One of Percy's favorite examples of rotation is the change in feeling one achieves by going to a western movie where the process of aesthetic impersonation takes place in identifying with the hero. One escapes the ordinary everydayness of his life for a moment as he lives-over into the new and exciting life of the lonely plainsman. The characteristic pattern of the western movie involves a "stranger dropping off the stagecoach into a ritual adventure before moving on" (*MB*, 93). Rotation can occur in many ways: by a chance meeting of "her," by a city dweller taking a trip to the Arizona desert, in short, by any kind of "getting clean away." The ultimate rotation, says Percy, is amnesia.

Angelism

The above are ways in which, by becoming absorbed in something in our environment external to ourselves, we escape or at least anesthetize, "the aching wound of self." The other main movement of evasion, that of giving ourselves over to abstractions, is a little more difficult to grasp. This is what Kierkegaard refers to as a "poet existence" and what Percy sometimes calls "angelism." This movement tends to take one away from an active involvement with the real world of which he is a part and into the world of abstractions. [The absent-minded professor is a caricature of this basic movement.] However, this should not allow us to suppose that we do not also share the tendency to let notions, ideas, or abstractions take the place of the real world for us. We do this because to do so is less painful than coping with the real. To treat someone as a category or an instance of a certain theory, for example, is much easier than being in contact with a difficult person.

Percy believes that this way of evading life is particularly pernicious in the modern era because of the impact of the scientific world-view on our consciousness (*MB*, 113). Science fosters in us a tendency to regard theory as more real than any particular we see around us. As Dr. Sutter Vaught of Percy's *The Last Gentleman* notes rather elliptically in his casebook:

> Man, who falls victim to transcendence as the spirit of abstraction, i.e., elevates self to posture over and against world which is *pari passu* demoted to immanence and seen as examplar and specimen and coordinate . . . (*TLG*, 331).

He had written before of the "displacement of the Real," a casebook reference to Alfred North Whitehead's description of the tendency—fostered by scientific objectivity—to mistake the abstract for the concrete. It is primarily the lay persons in a scientistic world who fall victim to this fallacy, not the scientists themselves. We absorb "the magical aura of science, whose credentials, we accept, for all sectors of reality" (*MB*, 113). We have trouble seeing persons in their unformulable depth and complexity, and tend to see them as examples of this or that category—successful executive, repairman, sales clerk, *et cetera*. Percy suggests that "the objective-biological concept of human life not only fails to apprehend but may actually worsen man's predicament in the world" (*Amer*, 415). He sees the central question of the European existentialists as being, "What is it like to be a man in a world transformed by science?" (*Shen*, 6)

The powerful impact of scientism on our consciousness, says Percy, "arouses in the modern novelist the deepest forebodings and at the same time kindles excitement and hope" (*MB*, 111). Even more portentious, he believes, than the new weapons that mankind has devised is "what is less apparent, a comparable realignment of energies within the human psyche. The psychical forces presently released in the post-modern consciousness open unlimited possibilities for both destruction and liberation, for an absolute loneliness or a rediscovery of community and reconciliation" (*MB*, 112). Like the French existentialist Gabriel Marcel he is much concerned with the possibility of a major catastrophe befalling mankind, and he sees the tendancy to abstraction as the primary devil in the piece. Marcel calls the "spirit of abstraction" the "root problem of our time," and describes it as follows:

> The more I emphasize the objectivity of things, thus cutting the umbilical cord which binds them to existence and to what has been termed my psycho-organic presence to myself, the more I affirm the independence of the world from me, its radical indifference to my destiny, to my goals; the more, too, this world, proclaimed as the only real one, is converted into an illusory spectacle, a great documentary film presented for my curiosity but ultimately abolished simply because it disregards me (CF, 21).

The potentiation of despair which results from alienation from our world may be the thing that can finally enable our breaking out of this form of aesthetic immediacy to the possibility of becoming sovereign beings. It is for this reason that the alienated post-modern consciousness may be called both fearful and hopeful.

Two examples from Percy's philosophical articles may further elucidate the problem of abstraction before we go on to see how this occurs in Percy's fictional characters. The essence of the problem, in Percy's view, is a loss of the ability to see and to be related to what we see by symbolizing it or articulating it for ourselves. Our minds, he believes, are dominated by symbolic complexes that come to us from the outside: from the "experts," through the media, and through the views of others. These pre-formed ideas, foisted upon us by a science-trusting society, prevent our own crucial act of formulating or understanding what we see. A partition exists between our eyes and what is out there. "It is only on the rarest occasions," says Percy, "that one may see his own hand" (MB, 88).

Why, for example, asks Percy, is it almost impossible really to see and appreciate the Grand Canyon in all its splendor in the same way that I can see a strange object I pick up in my own backyard?

It is almost impossible because the Grand Canyon, the thing as it is, has been appropriated by the symbolic complex which has already been formed in the sightseer's mind. Seeing the Canyon under approved circumstances is seeing the symbolic complex head on. The thing is no longer the thing as it confronted the Spaniard; it is rather that which has already been formulated— by picture postcard, geography book, tourist folders, and the words *Grand Canyon*. As a result of this preformulation, the source of the sightseer's pleasure undergoes a shift. Where the wonder and delight of the Spaniard arose from his penetration of the thing itself, from a progressive discovery of depths, patterns, colors, shadows, etc., now the sightseer measures his satisfaction *by the degree to which the Canyon conforms to the preformed complex* (*MB*, 47).

Things are prepackaged and arranged for us so that we lose the ability to see them. He notes that one could see the Canyon if he approached it from off the beaten track or if some catastrophe should happen while he was there which would break down the facilities designed to help him but which, in fact, undermine his own seeing.

Percy adds the example of a couple who get lost driving from Guanajuato to Mexico City and find themselves in a tiny valley, not on the map, and eventually in an Indian village. Some sort of religious festival is going on—apparently a corn dance in supplication of the rain god. They know at once that "this is it" and are entranced; they stay several days. Yet, asks Percy, do they really see the sight and come away rewarded? Do they have an immediate encounter with something real? The chances are, he says, that they will be strangely restless, feeling that this is too good to be true. Their remark later to their ethnologist friend back home provides the clue: " 'How we wished you could have been there with us!' " What they really wanted him for was not to share their experience, Percy says, but to "certify it as genuine."

What has taken place here, as in the case of the sightseers at the Grand Canyon, says Percy, is "a radical loss of sovereignty over that which is as much theirs as it is the ethnologist's . . . Sovereignty has been surrendered by the couple." This sort of surrender of sovereignty by the layman to the expert pervades our way of being in the world today. We become passive consumers of prepackaged, objectivized being, rather than active participants in the ever new discovery of things and persons. This cuts the roots of our participation in the real world and, to use Percy's expressive language, takes us into an "orbit of transcendence" from which it is very difficult to achieve reentry. The loss has come about, then, says Percy, "as the consequence of the seduction of the layman by science." Modern man, in a measure beyond that of his ancestors, tends not to experience himself as the owner of his own power and uniqueness of being but as an emptied-out thing, dependent on powers and factors outside himself.

Insofar as persons fail to deal with the tenuousness and pain of being wayfarers, by slipping into either "beastism" or "angelism," they are in despair, says Percy. The one is Kierkegaard's "despair of the lack of infinitude" and the other that of the "lack of finitude" (SD, 163–8). Movement in either direction is evasive and taken in order to feel safe. But "the worst of all despairs," says Percy, "is to imagine one is at home when one is really homeless" (MB, 144).

Percy believes the resulting malaise is widespread. We recall his remark that though the typical middle-aged American has been reasonably successful in providing a home and meeting the expectations of his family and peers, "His only problem now is to keep from blowing his brains out" (Ibid., 112). The feeling may only be the vague one that "something is wrong"; however, the most serious case of all is when one is not even aware that anything *is* wrong:

> One is, as the expression goes, fat, dumb, and happy. Though he lives the most meaningless sort of life, a trivial routine of meals, work, gossip, television, and sleep, he nevertheless feels quite content with himself and is at home in the world (Ibid., 134).

As the epigraph to his first novel Percy selected Kierkegaard's unsettling remark, "The specific character of despair is precisely this: it is unaware of being despair."

Chapter 4

Percy's Fictional "Dead"—I

W hile the theories set forth in his essays are central to Percy's understanding of how we fail to be the sovereign beings we are meant to be, it is in his fiction that we see it most clearly. Nowhere in his writings does he better describe the "death" in our living than he does in a brief section in his latest novel, *The Second Coming*. Here he sets forth various manifestations of the death in life, the self-loss.

Will Barrett, the hero of *The Second Coming*, is in passage through what might seem merely a mid-life crisis but is, at a deeper level, the crisis point in his search for self and God. At the time in which we come upon him he is becoming more and more aware of what he sees—what is happening with people.

Ha, there is a secret after all, he said. But to know the secret answer, you must first know the secret question. The question is, who is the enemy?

Not to know the name of the enemy is already to have been killed by him.

Ha, he said, dancing, snapping his fingers and laughing and hooting *ha hoo hee*, jumping up and down and socking himself, *but I do know. I know. I know the name of the enemy.*

The name of the enemy is *death*, he said, grinning and shoving his hands in his pockets. Not the death of dying but the living death . . . Why do men settle so easily for lives which are living deaths? Men either kill each other in war, or in peace walk as docilely into living death as sheep into a slaughterhouse (*SC*, 271).

Will has come to the point of seeing and articulating the fact that death is the enemy, and by that act he has begun to overcome it. "Not to know the name of the enemy is already to have been killed by him." Will is experiencing the same joy Helen Keller felt at her miraculous discovery that the wet substance she touched *was* water. She had named it, and in Percy's view had thereby moved from a kind of non-existence into human existence.

What is death-in-life, then? A few examples, ones perhaps not apparent in our vision, may make possible a sharing of Will's joy as we share in his naming.

> Here are the names of death which shall not prevail over me because I know the names.
>
> Death in the guise of love shall not prevail over me. You, old father, old mole, loved me but loved death better and in the name of love sought death for both of us . . .
>
> Death in the guise of Christianity is not going to prevail over me. If Christ brought life, why do the churches smell of death?
>
> Death in the guise of old Christendom in Carolina is not going to prevail over me. The old churches are houses of death.
>
> Death in the form of the new Christendom in Carolina is not going to prevail over me. If the born again are the twice born, I'm holding out for a third go-round . . .
>
> Death in the form of isms and asms shall not prevail over me, orgasm, enthusiasm, liberalism, conservatism, Communism, Buddhism, Americanism, for an ism is only another way of despairing of the truth.
>
> Death in the guise of marriage and family and children is not going to prevail over me. What happened to marriage and family that it should have become a travail and a sadness, marriage till death do us part yes but long dead before the parting, home and fireside and kiddies such a travail and a deadliness as to make a man run out into the night with his hands over his head? Show me that Norman Rockwell picture of the American family at Thanksgiving dinner and I'll show you the first faint outline of the death's-head (*SC*, 272–3).

32

Too pessimistic? Not when one understands that Percy passionately believes in life, and that his central thesis has to do with how one can be enabled to find it.

Percy agrees with Kierkegaard that the despair being evaded in the aesthetic mode of existence is "the sickness unto death" and that whatever enables one to avoid dealing with this sickness is also of the order of death. Evasion consists of sliding along on the surface, living only in the moment of immediate gratification in whatever form. It consists in not sufficiently detaching from the on-going flux of consumerism and pretense to see what is going on in and about oneself, to "name" it, and to act.

CONSUMERS

The most glaring examples of death-in-life in Percy's fiction appear in his fourth novel, *Lancelot*. In this book the "death" that the protagonist Lancelot sees in Margot, his wife, and her hedonistic friends was the immediate cause of his falling into a desperate and violent act of arson and murder. The fury of this act may reflect the depth of Percy's own revulsion at the death he sees as pervasive in our age.

Margot is a Texas girl, the daughter of a self-made millionaire oil man who had moved to New Orleans to make yet more money. She had aspirations for the good life when she trapped and married Lancelot, a middle-aged widower lawyer, scion of an aristocratic southern family, and slightly seedy inhabitant of what is left of the family plantation. Her particular aestheticism is soon apparent. She has gotten what she had always wanted—a beautiful old house and an "interesting" husband, whom she insists on dressing in the style of a southern gentleman. Her mode of the "beastly" movement into death is that of the consumer of the "good things" that she acquires—interesting husband, old home. Lance as a person is as invisible and as unnecessary to her as a stick of furniture:

> Later Margot, discovering that the pigeonnier was an architectural gem, had it converted into a study for me. To her delight,

after scraping off 150 years of pigeon shit they found the original cypress floor of two-by-twelves marvelously preserved, two-foot-thick walls of slave brick—even pigeons lived better than we do now. She found me a plantation desk and chair made by slave artisans and there I sat, feeling like Jeff Davis at Beauvoir, ready to write my memoirs. Except I had no memoirs. There was nothing to remember (*L*, 18).

Margot's consuming nature is traced even more clearly:

Later we lived by sexual delights and the triumphs of architectural restoration. Truthfully, at that time I don't know which she enjoyed more, a good piece in Henry Clay's bed or Henry Clay's bed. Once a couple of years ago when we were making love, I saw her arm stretch back in a way she had, but now not to grab the bedpost as a point of anchorage or leverage in the storm-tossed sea of love, to hold on for dear life—no, not at all: this time as her arm stretched up her fingers explored the fine oiled restored texture of the mahogany, her nails traced the delicate fluting of the heavy columns.

Later than that, when I took to the bottle—a different love story—and became a poor lover, once again inattentive and haunted, she came to prefer restoration to love. Certain architectural triumphs became for her like orgasms (*L*, 119).

But this is only the beginning of the path of dissolution for Margot. It is her steady but sure movement deeper into self-gratification that finally drives Lance to his violent deed. A movie company has contracted to use Belle Isle, Lance's plantation home, as the location for a film. The producer-director, Merlin, takes women where he can find them, as does Jacoby, the co-director, and other assorted members of the cast and film crew. The women, including Lance's daughter Lucy, are no different—the lust for sex has mastered them all, group sex and individual sex, heterosexual sex and homosexual sex.

I didn't think Raine was wonderful (as his daughter Lucy did). She was amazingly pretty, with a pure heart-shaped face and violet-cobalt eyes which seemed to look from her depths into yours, a trick I came to learn, that steady violet gaze, chin resting on the back of her bent hand. Her depths were vacant.

> But she flirted with me, and that was pleasant. Her single enthusiasm, beside her niceness, was her absorption with a California cult called IPD, or something like that—Ideo-Personal-Dynamics maybe (*Ibid.*, 111).

Margot is soon having an affair with Merlin and loving the excitement of it, and of her imagined coming into her own as an actress. The tone of hedonistic consumption of bodies and ego lusts is painted subtly but chillingly. The epigraph which Percy chose for the book is a fitting summation of its theme—human deadness in the extreme—and how the protagonist reacted to it.

> He sank so low that all means
> for his salvation were gone,
> except showing him the lost people.
> For this I visited the region of the dead.
>
> Dante, *Purgatorio*

The aesthetic mode of existence also takes less extreme forms, of course. Some of these Percy portrays with touches of irony and humor; however, the seriousness with which he views the condition is unmistakable.

It is the "comfortable predictable bourgeoise," on whom Percy focuses his attention in his first novel, *The Moviegoer*, who are trapped in "deadness." The story is about how the hero, Binx Bolling, is enabled to take certain steps to break out of that deadness into a "search" and eventually to the recovery of his self. The story is set in New Orleans after the Korean War and covers one significant week prior to Binx's thirtieth birthday. The protagonist is from an old New Orleans family on the side of his father, a "failed doctor" who sought to overcome his alienation by the "rotation" of joining the Royal Canadian Air Force at the outbreak of the Second World War and was soon killed. Like Binx, he was not at one with his world, but unlike Binx he never accomplished the task of becoming a self. Binx's mother, a former nurse, practical, earthy and not of the New Orleans elite, married a man more like herself after Binx's father's death and now lives with her younger children in a lake cottage near New Orleans. Binx was raised by his Aunt

Emily, his father's sister, and his Uncle Jules, who are typical old-family New Orleans.

Aunt Emily lives as if she were still in the post-Civil War era of the South when Greek classicism was in vogue. Greek art and sculpture adorned the "better" homes, and an attitude of *noblesse oblige* characterized the life style. Emily's husband, Jules, is different. He is a canny Cajun businessman who enjoys the Tulane football team, the Mardi Gras, and other assorted "good things" of life.

Binx had first awakened to "the possibility of a search" while lying wounded in a ditch in Korea. After his return he found he could not endure the self-absorbed good life being pursued by his former army buddies, and moved out to the middle-class suburb of Gentilly as a self-employed investment broker: "And there I have lived ever since, solitary, and in a wonder, wondering day and night, never a moment without wonder" (*M*, 42). Binx has taken the first step of breaking with the dead.

With the exception of Binx and Kate, the love interest in *The Moviegoer*, the other characters in the story all portray, in one mode or another, the predominant ways in which people slide off life and fail to grasp it, name it, and live it. Let Eddie Lovell, a typical New Orleans businessman of the inner social circle of this old city, be accepted as Exhibit A. Binx runs into Eddie one morning downtown. Eddie is in his early forties and is close to Binx's family. Like Binx, he is in the investment business. His brother, Lyall, who was killed a few years previously in an automobile accident, had been engaged to Kate, Binx's future wife.

Eddie is typical of so many of his type—he is absorbed in interesting things around him but is almost completely nonreflective. He is typical, too, in his southern manner, brimming over with seeming interest in Binx and his family, but this is only a cultural mannerism. "When we shake hands and part, it seems to me that I cannot answer the simplest question about what has taken place."

> As I listen to Eddie speak plausibly and at length of one thing and another—business, his wife Nell, the old house they are redecorating—the fabric pulls together into one bright texture of

36

investments, family projects, lovely old houses, little theater readings and such. It comes over me: this is how one lives! My exile in Gentilly has been the worst kind of self-deception (*M*, 18).

Binx may or may not be ironic in his assessment here of his own "exile." In any event, he is not drawn into Eddie's deadness, unless possibly for the moment.

Eddie's chatter is of the same sort as that of Mr. Vaught in *The Last Gentleman*, the money-dominated, successful businessman whose talk "was not really talk at all."

> The engineer soon learned to pay no attention to him either: his talk was not talk at all, one discovered, that is, a form of communication to be attended to, but rather a familiar hum such as Lugurtha the cook made when she was making beaten biscuits (*TLG*, 181).

Dr. "Dusty" Rhodes in *Love in the Ruins* is similarly described by Percy as buzzing, making sounds, but not talking. Kierkegaard observed that Don Juan does not speak but, as the essence of sensuous immediacy, is "only musically audible." The parallel is unmistakable. One cannot speak when one cannot say "I." To do that one has to exist as a self. In recalling his conversation with Eddie later in the week, Binx makes a penetrating observation which, like a similar one in Kierkegaard, cannot be taken lightly in spite of its tone. He says:

> For some time now the impression has been growing upon me that everyone is dead.
> It happens when I speak to people. In the middle of a sentence it will come over me: yes, beyond a doubt this is death. At such times it seems that the conversation is spoken by automatons who have no choice in what they say. I hear myself or someone else saying things like: "In my opinion the Russian people are a great people, but—"or "Yes, what you say about the hypocrisy of the North is unquestionably true. However—"and I think to myself: this is death. Lately it is all I can do to carry on such everyday conversations because my cheek has developed a tendency to twitch of its own accord. Wednesday as I stood speaking to Eddie Lovell, I felt my eye closing in a broad wink (*M*, 99).

Percy thus portrays the evasive human tendency to mouth clichés as one represses the inner urge to express one's self. To slip into this kind of retreat from responsibility is to let one's self atrophy by default. Kierkegaard, in a vein very similar to that used here by Percy, speaks of the dread feeling that sometimes comes over him in a conversation on the street when he begins to feel that he is talking to a walking stick with a talking machine mounted in its head.

> If you meet someone who suffers from such a derangement of feeling, the derangement consisting in his not having any, you listen to what he says in a cold and awful dread, scarcely knowing whether it is a human being who speaks, or a cunningly contrived walking stick, in which a talking machine had been concealed. . . . To find oneself engaged in rational and philosophical conversation with a walking stick is almost enough to make a man lose his mind (CUP, 175).

Eddie Lovell is wholly absorbed in the process of doing business and making money, and he is totally in tune with that process.

> Yes! Look at him. As he talks, he slaps a folded newspaper against his pants leg and his eye watches me and at the same time sweeps the terrain behind me, taking note of the slightest movement. A green truck turns down Bourbon Street; the eye sizes it up, flags it down, demands credentials, waves it on. A businessman turns in at the Maison Blanche building; the eye knows him, even knows what he is up to. And all the while he talks very well. His lips move muscularly, molding words into pleasing shapes, marshalling arguments and during the slight pauses are held poised, attractively everted in a Charles Boyer pout—while a little web of saliva gathers in a corner like the clear oil of a good machine. Now he jingles the coins deep in his pocket. No mystery here!—he is as cogent as a bird dog quartering a field. He understands everything out there and everything out there is something to be understood (M, 18).

Eddie is not only completely given over to what is going on "out there," but he instinctively (i.e., without the reflection that is distinctively human) assumes the necessary pose that impresses other people and thus will lead to success. What is external to him, out there in the environment, has been allowed to take over, and the self is not essentially functioning as such.

Eddie knows instinctively, through long practice, who is doing what out there; he is effortlessly attuned to picking up the signals and will just as spontaneously make his countermoves. He is victorious, and as long as things go well, his own reality never comes into the picture; in a real sense he does not have to will, decide, and act. He, like Don Juan, skips along the surface like a stone over the water, living only in the passing moment. Mr. Vaught is a businessman with the same kind of money-making immediacy.

> His talent, as the engineer divined it, was the knack of getting onto the rhythm of things, of knowing when to buy and sell. So that was the meaning of his funny way of hopping around like a jaybird with his ear cocked but not really listening to anybody! Rather was he tuned into the music and rhythm of ventures, himself poised and nodding, like a schoolboy waiting to go into a jump rope (*TLG*, 181).

What better description could be drawn of loss of self in the immediate absorption in externals?

It is also significant that "there is no mystery" in Eddie Lovell's view of things. To him everything is capable of being solved. He sees the other businessman as the opponent's piece in a chess game whose latest move is to be dealt with; he does not see him as an "unformulable" person. He is not open to the mystery around him but is intent upon solving his immediate problems and conflicts of success. His aura of success and confidence has the power to seduce another person, temporarily at least, just as does that of Don Juan. "It comes over me," says Binx, "this is how one lives! My exile in Gentilly has been the worst kind of self-deception."

Binx's Uncle Jules is the epitome of one who successfully covers up the anxiety that could lead to personal action by continually "consuming" that which is interesting, profitable, and productive of status. He has many and diverse interests and is admired by his friends. One of his lasting interests is the

Tulane football team. It has for some time been his "life ambition" to revive its fortunes. He dresses impeccably which may indicate to some extent the depth of his concerns:

> His shirt encases his body in a way that pleases me. It fits him so well. My shirts always have something wrong with them; they are too tight in the collar or too loose around the waist. Uncle Jules' collar fits his dark neck like a tape; his cuffs, folded like a napkin, just peep out past his coat sleeve; and his shirt front: the impulse comes over me at times to bury my nose in that snowy expanse of fine spun cotton (M, 30).

Binx also notes his "crop of thick gray hair cut short as a college boy's." One is reminded of the way in which clothes and rules of fashion dominate the lives of the women who patronize Kierkegaard's Ladies' Tailor (SLW, 80). Binx marvels that his uncle is "the only man I know whose victory in the world is total and unqualified." He has many friends, has made a lot of money, was Rex of Mardi Gras, gives freely of himself, and is an exemplary Catholic. The latter, says Binx, is hard to understand, "for the world he lives in, the City of Man, is so pleasant that the City of God must hold little in store for him" (M, 31).

When one looks behind this facade, however, it becomes clear that Jules has only marginal awareness of his own selfhood. "He has the gift of believing nothing can really go wrong in his household. . . . It is his confidence in Aunt Emily (his wife)." Jules believes that as long as Emily is mistress of the house even death itself is "nothing more than seemly." He thus lives on her strength and not out of himself. Emily's strong personality and habit of transfiguring members of her family into acceptable figures in her southern, stoic tradition has Jules seeing himself "as the Creole Cato, the last of the heroes—whereas the truth is that Uncle Jules is a canny Cajun straight from Bayou Lafourche, as canny as a Marseilles merchant and a very good fellow, but no Cato." He does not become really engaged with people; he "will neither trespass nor be trespassed upon. His armour is his unseriousness." Thus Jules fails to appropriate his own selfhood as an acting and responsible person. He lives for the pleasure of the moment and with the aid of props that are external to him, yet his apparent victory in the world is complete. One can almost hear the music of Don Giovanni surging through him.

IMPERSONATORS

Margot, Eddy, and Uncle Jules evade their selfhood by consuming such things as financial success, clothes, antiques, and other externals. The other chief way of evasion in Percy's view, that of impersonation, is amusingly portrayed in *The Moviegoer* in the person of Walter Wade. To impersonate is to pretend that one is something one is not in order to be acceptable. Thus one lives not his own self but another's. Walter was Binx's "big brother" in their college fraternity and is now a lawyer in New Orleans and about to become engaged to Kate.

An impersonator is, of course, other-directed, continually tuning his radar, on tiptoe to pick up signals from his social surroundings in order to be what is expected. This is Walter's orientation in life. We first meet him at lunch at Aunt Emily's where we find him with radar tuned. "Walter Wade cocks an ear and listens intently. He has not yet caught on to the Bollings' elliptical way of talking." In a little while he is certain of himself, "gets a raffish gleam in the eye" and ventures a remark. Unfortunately the remark was premature, however, and Aunt Emily is onto him. "Walter's eyes grow wider and warier, his smile more wolfish—he looks like a recruit picking his way through a mine field," so concerned is he to find the acceptable self to project at the moment (M, 31–4).

After lunch Walter approaches Binx alone about taking part in one of the Mardi Gras Krewes. "There is an exhilaration in his voice which carries over from his talk with Uncle Jules"; it may be presumed that he would not have had the exhilaration on his own. He says, " 'We've got a damn good bunch of guys now,' " and Binx reflects that ten years ago he would have said " 'ace gents'; that was what we called good guys in the nineteen forties." Walter has not changed since college days, when he was looked up to as the arbiter of taste:

> Walter still dresses as well as he did in college and sits and stands and slouches with the same grace. He still wears thick socks summer and winter to hide his thin veined ankles and still crosses his legs to make his calf look fat. (Ibid., 35)

When he was tapped for Golden Fleece, the highest of his collegiate honors, he confided to Binx: " 'The main thing, Binx, is to be humble, to make Golden Fleece and be humble about it.' " Thus his impersonations multiply.

One of Walter's hobbies at the time of the narrative is a houseboat which he and some of his friends, including Binx, had fixed up several years ago as a private hunting and fishing lodge.

> Walter liked nothing better than getting out in that swamp on week-ends with five or six fellows, quit shaving and play poker around the clock. He really enjoyed it. He would get up groaning from the table at three o'clock in the morning and pour himself a drink and, rubbing his beard, stand looking out into the darkness. "Goddamn, this is all right, isn't it? Isn't this a terrific set-up, Binx?" (Ibid., 39)

Walter adopts the camouflage of the macho sportsman, but it is clear that it is only an adoption and not the real thing. When Binx, asserting his own selfhood, admits to himself "to tell the truth I like women better," and does not respond to Walter's attempt to bring him back to the old group, Walter strikes another pose in order to attune himself to Binx's stance: " 'No, you're right. What would we talk about,' says Walter elegiacally, 'Oh Lord. What's wrong with the goddamn world, Binx?' " (Ibid., 39).

Thus Walter is an impersonator. He is only outdone by an even less subtle poser—Sam Yerger, a former world-traveling journalist, now popular novelist and intimate of the family. Sam speaks like a character out of a Hemingway book: " 'She's a fine girl. Always cherish your woman, Binx' " This has become a cliché with him and he repeats it on various occasions. During a family discussion concerning the seriously ailing Kate, Sam, who has come in from New York as the one who can help, stands placing "heel to toe and holding his elbow in his hand and his arm straight up and down in front of him—himself gathered to a point, aimed—puffs a cigarette" (Ibid., 171). He takes obvious pleasure in being the called-in family expert as he tells the others of Kate's attempted suicide the night before. In the midst of the discussion Aunt Emily calls and again Sam reveals his overriding concern for his image:

> "Sam!" My aunt's voice, low and rich in overtones of meaning, comes down to us.
> Sam looks down past his arm to see that his heel is aligned properly. (Ibid., 173)

Percy's self-appraisal as one who has a "nose for the merde" seems amply borne out in descriptions of this kind. Sam's concern for his own image, in this and in other less obvious but more crucial instances, effectively prevents his being sufficiently aware to help Kate. Thus again, to be absorbed in externals, in this case of living a false self, can prevent any I-Thou relationship which could itself be the cure for such deathly impersonation.

A way of impersonation that Percy sees as being characteristic of Americans in general is the pervading "niceness" of almost everyone. As Dr. More in *Love in the Ruins* returns from the mental ward, where he has been a patient, to the outside world and begins to meet people, he says, "The niceness is terrifying . . . the abyss yawns" (*LIR*, 107). Again and again in the novels people are ironically described in such terms as "triumphs of niceness" and "alike as peas in a pod" (*M*, 108–9). He sees Americans today as indulging simultaneously in "two American dreams: of Ozzie and Harriett, nicer-than-Christian folks, and of Tillie and Mac and belly to back," the latter referring to surreptitious sex fantasy and action (Ibid., 207). To be "nice" is to live outside oneself, because the self is not really so nice. It is terrifying because one never knows what is beneath the mask (*LIR*, 87).

Impersonations appear by the score in *The Moviegoer*. One example, worthy of at least passing note because it is so typical, rounds out the picture of the Lovell couple. Binx runs into

Nell Lovell at the library one day, where she approaches him angrily brandishing a celebrated novel which takes a somewhat pessimistic view of things.

> "I don't feel a bit gloomy!" she cries. "Now that Mark and Lance have grown up and flown the coop, I am having the time of my life. I'm taking philosophy courses in the morning and working nights at Le Petite Theatre. Eddie and I have reexamined our values and found them pretty darn enduring. To our utter amazement we discovered that we both have the same life-goal. Do you know what it is?"
> "No."
> "To make a contribution, however small, and leave the world just a little better off" (*M*, 101).

This is an image which, in Nell's view, everyone would have to agree is the highest that could be imagined in the context of modern Western humanism. Nell and Eddie are desperately attempting to achieve this ideal, thinking thereby to attain reality.

> "That's very good," I say somewhat uneasily and shift about on the library steps. I can talk to Nell as long as I don't look at her. Looking into her eyes is an embarrassment.
> "—we gave the television to the kids and last night we turned on the hi-fi and sat by the fire and read *The Prophet* aloud. I don't find life gloomy!" she cries. "To me, books and people and things are endlessly fascinating. Don't you think so?"
> "Yes." A rumble has commenced in my descending bowel, heralding a tremendous defecation. (Ibid., 101)

Nell and Eddie refuse to see anything gloomy about the world, preferring to abstract out of the real world in an impersonation that is regarded by themselves and others as commendable—giving up the TV set, listening to good music and reading *The Prophet* aloud before the fire! "Yes, true," says Binx, "Values. Very good. And then I can't help wondering to myself: why does she talk as if she were dead? Another forty years to go and dead, dead, dead." (Ibid., 102)

Chapter 5

Percy's Fictional "Dead"—II

We turn now to the characters who portray the other primary way Percy sees people losing sovereignty over their lives. This is the tendency, accentuated in this age of science, to be dominated by abstractions and thus alienated from the environment of persons and things. This tendency is what Percy and Kierkegaard have termed "angelism" or "intellectual immediacy."

Angelism, as both writers see it, has two forms, which may overlap: a person can *passively* fall into abstraction, as in the earlier example of vacationers unable to see the Grand Canyon; or, one can *actively* seek the abstract realm of ideas and "answers," as did Kierkegaard's Faust. The more common of the two is to fall passively into the prevailing ideas and abstractions which dominate one's culture. Percy's writings are full of characterizations of this form of angelism. They are usually portrayed humorously but with an underlying sadness and irony because of the personal loss such a "falling" entails. We shall look at some of his specific examples.

The way of actively seeking life in ideas and abstractions is more pernicious than the passive way and can lead to severe forms of isolation. Percy portrays this Faustian movement most distinctly in Dr. Sutter Vaught in *The Last Gentleman*. It can be said, however, that the tendency afflicts all of his protagonists, and it is from it that they are finally saved. Percy can write so vividly about it because, no doubt, it is his own affliction as it is that of most intellectuals.

More than likely, Dr. Thomas More is speaking Percy's thoughts in the following humorous soliloquy, as he examines a patient with his new invention for detecting levels of abstraction in patients.

> He registered a dizzy 7.6 mmv over Brodmann 32, the area of abstractive activity. Since that time I have learned that a reading over 6 generally means that a person has so abstracted himself from himself and from the world around him, seeing things as theories and himself as a shadow, that he cannot, so to speak reenter the lovely ordinary world. Instead he orbits the earth and himself. Such a person, and there are millions, is destined to haunt the human condition like the Flying Dutchman . . . Over his coeliac plexus, soothed though he was, he still clocked a thunderous anxiety of 8.7 mmv. His hand trembled slightly against mine. And all at once I could see how he lived his life: shuddering in orbit around the great globe, seeking some way to get back. Don't I know? We are two of a kind, winging it like Jupiter and spying comely maids below and having to take the forms of swans and bulls to approach them. Except that he, good heathen that he is, wished only to re-enter his own wife. I, the Christian, am the fornicator (*LIR*, 34–5).

PASSIVE ANGELISM

There are many ways in which a person may fall passively into domination by symbolic complexes external to the self. These are ideas and ways of looking at things that come from outside, from the cultural environment and, one tends to believe, are more to be trusted than one's own act of seeing. External symbols thus "hook" the person and take away his sovereign seeing and acting. Some fictional examples of this very common phenomenon follow.

Will Barrett

Let us look first at Will Barrett, the protagonist of *The Last Gentleman*. Will is a young Alabaman in his early 20s who has left Princeton, the college of his father and grandfather, in the fall of his junior year and is living alone in a Y.M.C.A. in New York City. He has already made certain significant choices by which he has begun what the author calls a "passionate quest" for recovery of himself.

> He was a young man of pleasant appearance. Of medium height and exceedingly pale, he was nevertheless strongly built and quick and easy in his ways . . . Handsome as he was, he was given to long silences. So girls didn't know what to make of him. But men liked him. After a while they saw that he was easy and meant no harm. . . . But he looked better than he was. Though he was as engaging as could be, something was missing. He had not turned out well (*TLG*, 8).

Will is afflicted by the tendency to abstraction in spite of the fact that he has begun the passionate quest and is seen by the author as being in Kierkegaard's religious mode of existence. This shows that angelism is an ever-present temptation from which no one is immune. But his slipping off into abstraction undermines his ability to act. The author wastes no time in stating this problem when Will is first introduced: "He was an unusual young man. But perhaps nowadays it is not so unusual. What distinguished him anyhow was this: he had to know everything before he could do anything."

Percy's view that this tendency is markedly increased today is brought out rather humorously in his portrayal of Will's forebears, beginning with his great grandfather:

> Over the years his family had turned ironical and lost its gift for action. It was an honorable and violent family, but gradually the violence had been deflected and turned inward. The great grandfather knew what was what and said so and acted accordingly and did not care what anyone thought. He even wore a pistol in a holster like a Western hero and once met the Grand Wizard of the Ku Klux Klan in a barbershop and invited him then and there to shoot it out in the street. The next generation, the grandfather, seemed to know what was what but he was not really so sure. He was brave but he gave much thought to the business of being brave. He too would have shot it out with the Grand Wizard if only he could have made certain it was the thing to do. The father was a brave man too and he said he didn't care what others thought, but he did care. More than anything

else, he wished to act with honor and to be thought well of by other men. So living for him was a strain. He became ironical. (Ibid., 9)

Excessive reflection, the consideration of interminable possibilities, the need to make certain that this is "the thing to do," all, in Percy's view, have progressively atrophied the person's ability to act so that "often nowadays people do not know what to do and live out their lives as if they were waiting for some sign or other." To be so immobilized and to have one's life dependent upon the external approval of some unseen expert or authority is increasingly the plight of man in mass society, Percy believes.

The sickness becomes acute in Will from time to time, especially when the abstracting tendencies of other people impinge upon him. At these times he slips into a "fugue state" which frequently culminates in complete amnesia. As a youth he had lived in a "state of liveliest expectation," looking forward to becoming a man when he would "know what to do," but his life had not turned out that way. "For some years he had had a nervous condition and as a consequence he did not know how to live his life." Sometimes he was quite normal. He knew from the experts on human relations what could lead to the good life: "that it is people who count . . . one's warmth toward and understanding of people." Most of the time, however, "he would lapse into an unproductive and solitary life." Most of his life was a "gap." "The summer before he had fallen into a fugue state and wandered around northern Virginia for three weeks, where he sat sunk in thought on old battlegrounds, hardly aware of his own name" (Ibid., 10–12).

In his presentation of Will, Percy has, of course, purposely exaggerated to show his view of how science and a mass society have affected the consciousness of modern people. He embodies in his fictional characters various forms taken by the perennial "sickness unto death" in present-day Western culture. We shall look at several of these, beginning with the way in which Will is particularly affected. It is clear throughout, however, that Will, in his detachment from the crowd and in his search for meaning, "sick" as he sometimes seems, is healthy in the author's view, compared to those whose life consists of being warm and understanding toward people.

We are told that Will's "trouble came from groups. . . . He had trouble doing what the group expected him to do." We note immediately that the problem is one of choice, of decision and action. Percy is saying that it is the same trouble that Will's grandfather and father were beginning to experience vis-a-vis the great-grandfather; namely, the intrusion of a debilitating reflection whereby one must make certain of the proper thing to do before doing it. Why is this worse in a culture dominated by the abstracting habit of mind which science fosters? Percy suggests that intervening between Will and the group in which he is placed is a tendency to think that there is a certain ideal or universal form for human relationships. If he can himself appropriate this approved way of being with others, he will find personal fulfillment; he will in effect say, "this is it!" This habit of mind, Percy insists, subtly pervades everyone's thinking today and is rooted in the layman's misapplication of science, which tends to regard theory as more real than the concrete entity it attempts to explain. (Alfred North Whitehead called this fall into abstraction the "fallacy of misplaced concreteness.") For example, Will's trouble with groups is only aggravated by his consultations with his psychiatrist. This "expert" theorizes and leads Will to theorize about his role in the group. As a result Will has worked so hard at role-taking under the influence of the expert's advice "that he would tend to all but disappear into the group," to become identical with the various roles suggested to him. "As a consequence this young man, dislocated to begin with, hardly knew who he was from one day to the next" (*TLG*, 19).

What has happened is that, instead of being directly related to the others and responding as a self to them, he has surrendered his own sovereignty to the expert, who has led him to see these other people as abstract players of roles and himself in the same way. Essentially the same thing has happened as happens to the tourist who does not see the Grand Canyon but the idea of what it is supposed to be, what it means, what it represents as posited by the experts. Scien*tism* and the media tend to seduce us from our perception of and relationship to our environment and other people. We come to rely on "experts" in many areas of our lives.

Will recalls an incident in summer camp when he was a boy:

> Now here was one group, the campers, he had no use for at all. The games and the group activities were a pure sadness. One night as the tribe gathered around the council fire to sing songs and listen to the director tell stories and later ask everyone to stand up then and there and make a personal decision for Christ, he crept out of the circle of firelight and lit out down the road to Asheville . . . and hitchhiked the rest of the way home (Ibid., 13).

The expert in this case is the camp leadership that superimposes the accepted image of "tribe" on the life of the camp and the relationships between campers. Will is expected to conform to a preconceived pattern. If he is to be an acceptable camper, he is expected to see tribal categories like chief, squaw, and brave instead of the concrete realities of his buddies, Bill, Joe and Jack. There are the tribal council fire, songs, and stories and even the need, if he is to meet expectations, to "stand up then and there and make a personal decision for Christ." The "pure sadness" lies in the phoniness of it all. That this was Will's feeling is indicated by the way in which he spent the rest of the summer. He moved completely away from any superimposition of roles by spending the summer with a black friend, "aloft, reading comics" in a tree house they had built "tossed like a raft in a sea of dappled leaves."

Years later at Princeton, Will again experiences difficulty in groups. These were supposed to be the best years of their lives, and so it seemed to most. But one had to mold oneself to the idealized Princeton image which had evolved and been lived by these young men's fathers and grandfathers and thus had the authority of tradition.

> They had a certain Princeton way of talking, even the ones from Chicago and California, and a certain way of sticking their hands in their pockets and settling their chins in their throats. They were fine fellows, though, once you got used to their muted Yankee friendliness. Certainly this was the best of times he told himself with a groan (Ibid., 14).

One tends not to really "see" a fellow human being in all of his particularity in such a situation. One is separated from him by an idealized image, proclaimed to be the acceptable one, and thus one experiences alienation from reality and from one's self.

Sexual Relationships

The intrusion of the expert into the intimacy of the sexual relationship is another facet of modern life that is of particular concern to Percy. Binx Bolling, hero of *The Moviegoer*, is on a train with his soon-to-be fiancée, Kate, on their way to Chicago in a spur-of-the-moment flight from the heaviness of family expectations. He is sitting beside a fortyish, apparently successful businessman, a healthy and pleasant fellow on his way home to St. Louis. He is reading his newspaper and Binx cannot help noticing when "he takes out a slender gold pencil, makes a deft one-handed adjustment, and underlines several sentences with straight black lines (he is used to underlining). Dreaming at his shoulder, I can make out no more than:

In order to deepen and enrich the marital—

It is a counseling column which I too read faithfully" (*M*, 188–9). Obviously the man is used to underlining because, like most of us, he is in the habit of looking for what the experts can tell him about how to live.

As the train rocks along Binx finds himself in "waking, wide-eyed dreams":

Dr. and Mrs. Bob Dean autograph copies of their book *Technique in Marriage* in a Canal Street department store. A pair of beauties. I must have come in all the way from Gentilly, for I stand jammed against a table which supports a pyramid of books. I cannot take my eyes from the Deans: an oldish couple but still handsome and both, rather strangely, heavily freckled. As they wait for the starting time, they are jolly with each other and swap banter in the professional style of show people (I believe these preliminaries are called the warm-up). "No, we never argue," says Bob Dean. "Because whenever an argument starts, we consult the chapter I wrote on arguments." "No, dear," says Jackie Dean. "It was I who wrote the chapter—" etc. Everyone laughs. I notice that nearly all the crowd jamming against me are women, firm middle-aged one-fifty pounders. Under drooping lids I watch the Deans, peculiarly affected by their routine which is staged so effortlessly that during the exchange of quips, they are free to cast business-like looks about them as if no one were present. But when they get down to business, they become as sober as Doukhobors and effuse an air of dedicated almost evangelical helpfulness. A copy of the book lies open on the table. I read: "Now with a tender regard for your partner remove your hand from the nipple and gently manipulate—" It is impossible not to imagine them at their researches, as solemn as a pair of brontosauruses, their heavy old freckled limbs twined about each other, hands probing skillfully for sensitive zones, pigmented areolas, out-of-the-way mucous glands, dormant vascular nexuses. A wave of prickling passes over me such as I have never experienced before (*M*, 189–90).

What may happen between persons in the marital bed when cultural expectations and ideas take over is again humorously but sadly portrayed in an incident that takes place a little later in Kate's roomette.

We have to lie down: the door opens onto the bed . . .
Her black, spiky eyes fall full upon me, but not quite seeing, I think. Propped on one hand, she bites her lip and lets the other fall on me heavily, as if I were an old buddy. "I'll tell you something."
"What?"
"The other day I said to Merle." [Merle is her psychiatrist.] Again the hand falls heavily and takes hold of me. "What would you say to me having a little fling?" (Ibid., 198)

She is looking for "the real thing." She wants permission from her resident expert, Merle, and she hopes Binx will agree that this "plain old monkey business" that she intends to have with him *is* the sort of thing that is the real thing. With Kate, conditioned by relying on such expert certifiers, and with Binx under the kind of expectation imposed by Dr. and Mrs. Bob Dean, the sex manual writers, it is not surprising that the ensuing engagement was less than successful.

I'll have to tell you the truth, Rory, painful though it is. Nothing would please me more than to say that I had done one of two things. Either that I did what you do: tuck Debbie in your bed and, with a show of virtue so victorious as to be ferocious, grab pillow and blanket and take to the living room sofa, there to lie in the dark, hands clasped behind head, gaze at the ceiling and talk through the open door of your hopes and dreams. Or— do what a hero in a novel would do: he too is a seeker and a pilgrim of sorts and he is just in from Guanajuato or Sambuco where he has found the Real Right Thing or from the East where he apprenticed himself to a wise man and became proficient in the seventh path to the seventh happiness. Yet he does not disdain this world either and when it happens that a maid comes to his bed with a heart full of longing for him, he puts down his book in a good and cheerful spirit and gives her as merry a time as she could possibly wish for. Whereupon, with her dispatched into as sweet a sleep as ever Scarlett enjoyed the morning of Rhett's return, he takes up his book again and is in an instant ten miles high and on the Way.

No, Rory, I did neither. We did neither. We did very badly and almost did not do at all. Flesh poor flesh failed us. The burden was too great and flesh poor flesh . . . now at this moment summoned all at once to be all and everything, end all and be all, the last and only hope—quails and fails (*M*, 199–200).

Thus the images, ideas, and expectations imposed from the outside culture can get in the way of a relationship with the flesh-and-blood person at one's side.

If a direct relationship may be blocked by the intervention of external symbols, it can temporarily be recovered if these externals can somehow be swept away. This happens when something occurs to take one's mind off them. An example may help to identify the intellectual veils that too often separate us from our environment: Consider Will Barrett off on a weekend with a rather sophisticated young lady.

The summer before, he had got caught in hurricane Donna. A girl named Midge Auchincloss, none other in fact than the daughter of his father's old friend, had invited him to drive her up to a jazz festival in Newport. During the same weekend a small hurricane was beating up along the coast but giving every sign of careening off into the North Atlantic. Nobody took much notice of it. Friday afternoon, nothing was very different. The old Northeast smelled the same, the sky was hazed over, and things were not worth much. The engineer and his friend Midge behaved toward each other in their customary fashion. They did not have much to say, not as a consequence of breakdown in communications such as one often hears about nowadays, but because there was in fact not much to say. Though they liked each other well enough, there was nothing to do, it seemed, but press against each other whenever they were alone. Coming home to Midge's apartment late at night, they would step over the sleeping Irishman, stand in the elevator and press against each other for a good half hour, each gazing abstractedly and dry-eyed over the other's shoulder.

But a knoll of high pressure reared up in front of Donna and she backed off to the west. On the way home from Newport, the Auchinclosses' Continental ran into the hurricane in Connecticut. Searching for Bridgeport and blinded by the rain, which hit the windshield like a stream from a firehose, the engineer took a wrong exit off the turnpike and entered upon a maze of narrow high-crowned blacktops such as crisscross Connecticut, and got lost. Within a few minutes the gale winds reached near-hurricane strength and there was nothing to do but stop the car. Feeling moderately exhilarated by the uproar outside and the snugness within, dry as a bone in their cocoon of heavy-gauge metal and safety glass, they fell upon one another fully clothed and locked in a death grip. Strange Yankee bushes, perhaps alder and dogbane, thrashed against the windows. Hearing a wailing sound, they sat up and had the shock of their lives. There, standing in the full glare of the headlights, or rather leaning against the force of the hurricane, was a child hardly more than a babe. For a long moment there was nothing to do but gaze at him, so wondrous a sight it was, a cherub striding the blast, its cheeks puffed out by the four winds. Then he was blown away. The engineer went after him, backing up on all fours, butt to wind like a range pony, reached the ditch and found him. Now with the babe lying as cold as lard between them and not even shivering, the engineer started the Continental and crept along, feeling the margin of the road under his tire like a thread under the fingertip, and found a diner, a regular old-style streetcar of a restaurant left over from the days before the turnpikes.

For two hours they sat in a booth and cared for the child, fed him Campbell's chicken-and-rice soup and spoke to him. He was not hurt but he was round-eyed and bemused and had nothing to say. It became a matter of figuring out what to do with him. The phone was dead and there was no policeman or anyone at all except the counterman, who brought a candle and joined them. The wind shrieked and the streetcar swayed and thrummed as if its old motors had started up. A window broke. They helped the counterman board it up with Coca-Cola crates.

> Midge and the counterman, he noticed, were very happy. The
> hurricane blew away the sad, noxious particles which befoul the
> sorrowful old Eastern sky and Midge no longer felt obliged to
> keep her face stiff. They were able to talk (*TLG*, 22–24).

We may assume that the whole complex of preconceptions
in Will's mind arising from Midge being the daughter of his
father's well-to-do friend, along with her own need to fit a certain debutante image and "keep her face stiff," stood as a bar-
rier between them. The hurricane "blew away the sad, noxious
particles which befoul the sorrowful old Eastern sky and Midge
no longer felt obliged to keep her face stiff. They were able to
talk." What the hurricane had actually blown away for the
moment were the preformed symbolic complexes that had
separated Will and Midge from each other. Seeing her for the
first time in her flesh and blood reality, Will's inhibitions
disappear and he is enabled to act from his own sovereign self.
He can talk and so can she.

ACTIVE ANGELISM

Now we look at Percy's characterizations of that rather more
rare movement into abstraction, which a person undertakes actively. In both the passive and the active manifestations of
angelism, the movement is regressive, that is, *away* from involvement with the "ordinary lovely world" in which we live.
It is a retreat from the risks and anxieties of seeing and acting
on one's own. In this way one fails to insert himself into the
world and to shoulder the burden of his freedom. The attempt
to hide in the comfort and safety of the "aesthetic mode of existence" is at bottom an abandonment of life, hence, insofar as
a person does it, a living death. Angelism is universal in its
passive form. Its active form, however, is a temptation that ap-
peals to a more limited group, particularly to the intellectually
and spiritually inclined.

Perhaps the most striking example of active angelism, in
Kierkegaard's observation, is the philosopher G. W. F. Hegel.
Hegel was the dominant philosophical figure in Kierkegaard's
time. He had developed an all-encompassing philosophical

system to explain reality and believed that his system was the final truth after centuries of previous attempts on the part of philosophers. The only trouble, as Kierkegaard observed, was that Hegel's system, as magnificent as it was, left out of consideration the most important thing of all—the individual human person: it explained everything except how a person can live his life from one ordinary moment to the next. Kierkegaard likened Hegel's system to an imposing castle constructed as a man's life-work. The irony, he pointed out, is that the builder finds himself living in a little hut outside the castle walls. Hegel in his philosophical construct of a model of reality attempts to find his life in an abstraction, but he finds that his unformulable, individual deciding and acting self has no part in the system. His attempt to escape the world by moving into the sublime world of pure thought is frustrated. Kierkegaard's graphically portrayed Faust is such a personage. Faust attempts to escape the anxiety of choosing and acting in the world, but his evasion of real life leads him only deeper into despair.

Very few go the lengths of Hegel in this movement, if Kierkegaard interprets him correctly. However, most people fall into active angelism to some extent and in varying ways. We shall look first at two minor characters who clearly exhibit this movement, and then at a major character in whom the movement has advanced to dangerously debilitating lengths.

Elgin

In the age of science there is a tendency, among those so inclined, to seek reality in scientific abstractions. Elgin Buell, the black M.I.T. senior in *Lancelot*, is one such person. Elgin is the son of Ellis Buell who grew up with Lance as a child and whose family has been working for Lance's family for forty years.

> Elgin, age twenty-two, is a well-set-up youth, slim, cafe-au-lait, and smart—he went to St. Augustine, the elite Black Catholic school in New Orleans, knew more about chemistry than you and I learned in college. Then got a scholarship to M.I.T. He is well-spoken but to save his life he can't say *ask* any

more than a Japanese can say an *r* or a German *thank you*. If he becomes a U.S. Senator or wins the Nobel Prize, which he is more apt to do than you or I, he'll sure as hell say *ax* in his acceptance speech (*L*, 44).

Elgin is home for the summer, and he and his sister, Doreen, take turns leading tourists through Belle Isle. He plays an important part in Lance's detective work in uncovering Margot's affair with the director, Merlin, and both hers and their daughter's licentious behavior with the movie crew as a whole.

But Elgin has decided deficiencies as a human being. He seems to be a kind of a machine, devoid of human values.

> Elgin's expression did not change. The only sign of his surprise was that though his face was turned slightly away, head cocked as if he were deaf, his eyes never left mine and had a wary hooded look.
> "Elgin, I'm going to ask a favor of you."
> "Yes, sir."
> "It is not difficult. The point is, I want you to do it without further explanation on my part. Would you?"
> "Yes, sir," said Elgin without a change of tone or blink of eye. "Even if it's criminal or immoral"—slight smile now. "You know I'd do anything you axed" (Ibid., 91).

Elgin had "a lately acquired frowning finicky manner which irritated me a little just as it irritates me in a certain kind of scientist who does not know what he does not know and discredits more than he should."

> Elgin was one of them. It was as if he had sailed in a single jump from Louisianan pickaninny playing marbles under a chinaberry tree to a smart-ass M.I.T. senior, leapfrogging not only the entire South but all of history as well. And maybe he knew what he was doing. From cotton patch to quantum physics and glad not to have stopped along the way (Ibid., 92).

Percy is saying that Elgin abstracted himself out of concrete everyday life when he fell in love with science. For example, his father, Ellis, had recently been threatened by the Ku Klux Klan and had been defended by Lance, who was well acquainted with the Grand Kleagle from public school days. Ellis never tired of saying "you should have seen Mr. Lance call that white trash out." But:

> His son Elgin was a different matter. Actually Elgin was the only one who didn't care much one way or the other about such matters. Like Archimedes he was more interested, exclusively interested, in writing out his formulae and would not have cared or even noticed whether it was a Kluxer or a Roman soldier who lifted his hand against him.
>
> Elgin, I do believe, would do what I asked, not out of gratitude (a very bad emotion as both he and I knew), but because he liked me and felt sorry for me. Unlike him I had been unable to escape into the simple complexities of science. All he had to do was solve the mystery of the universe, which may be difficult but is not as difficult as living an ordinary life.
>
> I had counted too on my request intriguing him as a kind of mathematical game, which it was. It did (Ibid., 94).

To "escape into the simple complexities of science" is one manifestation of intellectual immediacy by which a person can opt out of living. There are certainly shades of Kierkegaard's polemic against Hegel here. The basic tendency can be seen in many in a science-oriented, computer age in which measurable quantities and scientific hypothesis are generally considered the only reality, while the intangibles of human relationship are downgraded in the public mind to the realm of the merely sentimental.

However, if a person can escape the real world into the "simple elegance" of the abstractions of science, one can also escape into the abstractions of the spirit; that is, what Kierkegaard once called a "poet existence." Percy speaks of music and beauty as a whore, just as he speaks with unconcealed disdain of those who pride themselves in reading the Great Books and seeking the "finer things of life." This again is the fallacy of actively seeking the "real thing" in elements that are abstracted out of life instead of in one's own place and through one's own acts.

Doris

A striking example of abstracting away from life into art and spiritualism is provided by Doris, Thomas More's ex-wife in

Love in the Ruins. Tom, the hero of that novel, is the slighty shaky, middle-aged psychiatrist who seems essentially to be in the religious mode of existence and who will be investigated as such in a later chapter.

The tip of Doris' iceburg as a drifter into "poet existence" reveals itself early in their marriage in her decision to name their daughter Samantha.

> My wife, an ex-Episcopal girl from Virginia, named our daughter Samantha in the expectation that this dark gracile pagan name would somehow inform the child, but alas for Doris, Samantha turned out to be chubby, fair, acned, and pious, the sort who likes to hang around after school and beat Sister's erasers (*LIR*, 12).

Later he reflects: "A description of my wife: the sort of woman who would name our daughter Samantha though there was no one in our families with this name" (Ibid., 62). The concreteness of their family and family history does not enter into the naming of their own child; only an abstract idea does. An indication of the society's loss of individual roots and of individuals moving into the abstract mass can be seen in the fads of child-naming: one need only think of the proliferation of Heathers, Dawns, Scotts and Andreas in our own time.

A fuller description of Doris and her active movement into angelism is provided in the following:

> Directly above my head on the glass-topped coffee table are Doris's favorite books just as she left them in the "enclosed patio." That was before I roofed it, and the books are swollen by old rains to fat wads of pulp, but still stacked so:
>> *Siddhartha*
>> *Atlas Shrugged*
>> *ESP and the New Spirituality*
> Books matter. My poor wife, Doris, was ruined by books, by books and a heathen Englishman, not by dirty books but by clean books, not by depraved books but by spiritual books. God, if you recall, did not warn his people against dirty books. He warned them against high places. My wife, who began life as a cheerful Episcopalian from Virginia, became a priestess of the high places. I loved her dearly and loved to lie with her and would and did whene'er she would allow it, but most especially

in the morning, at breakfast, in the nine o'clock sunlight out here on the "enclosed patio." But books ruined her. Beware of Episcopal women who take up with Ayn Rand and the Buddha and Dr. Rhine formerly of Duke University. A certain type of Episcopal girl has a weakness that comes on them just past youth, just as sure as Italian girls get fat. They fall prey to Gnostic pride, commence buying antiques, and develop a yearning for esoteric doctrine (Ibid., 64).

It was the twelve-year-old Samantha's death that left the vacancy in the marriage which Tom and Doris were never able to fill. When Samantha had been dead some months, "Doris began talking of going to the Isle of Jersey or New Zealand where she hoped to recover herself, learn quiet breathing in a simple place, etcetera, etcetera, perhaps in the bright shadow of a 'dobe wall or perhaps in a stone cottage under a great green fell." It is clear that she is moving into a world of clichés, captured by ideas engendered by her spiritual and poetic reading.

Tom has a hard time accommodating to the sadness of the loss of Doris to her abstractions. She was so physically present but so mentally and spiritually absent.

The morning sun, just beginning to slant down into the "enclosed patio," struck the top of her yellow hair, sending off fiery aureoles like sunflares. I never got over the splendor of her person in the morning, her royal green-lined-clad self, fragrant and golden-fleshed. Her flesh was gold amorphous stuff. Though it was possible to believe that her arm had the usual layers of fat, muscle, artery, bone, these gross tissues were in her somehow tranformed by her girl-chemistry, bejeweled by her double-X chromosome. Those were the days of short skirts, and she looked like long-thighed Mercury, god of morning. Her heels had wings. Her legs were long and deep-fleshed, bound laterally in the thigh by a strap of fascia that flattened the triceps. Was it her slight maleness, long-leggedness—perhaps 10 percent tunic-clad Mercury was she—that set my heart pounding over breakfast?

No, that's foolishness. I loved her, that's all.

"Where are you going?" I asked again, buttering the grits and watching her hair flame like the sun's corolla.

"I'm going in search of myself."

My heart sank. This was not really her way of talking. It was the one tactic against which I was defenseless, the portentous gravity of her new beliefs. When she was an ordinary ex-Episcopalian, a good-humored Virginia girl with nothing left of her religion but a fondness for old brick chapels, St. John o' the Woods, and the superb English of the King James Version, we had common ground.

"Don't leave, Doris," I said, feeling my head grow heavy and sink toward the grits.

"I have to leave. It is the one thing I must do."

"Why do you have to leave?"

"We're so dead, Tom. Dead inside. I must go somewhere and recover myself. To the lake isle of Innisfree."

"Jesus, let's go to the lake isle together."

"We don't relate any more, Tom" (Ibid. 65–6).

Not only the poesy but also the jargon-laden expectations of the marriage experts come between Tom and Doris and do their marriage in. In addition to books, other "spiritual" influences had entered Doris's life:

"But we don't relate," said Doris absently, still not leaving though, eyes fixed on Saint Francis who was swarming with titmice. "There are no overtones in our relationship, no nuances, no upper mansions. Build thee more stately mansions, O my soul."

"All right."

"It's not your fault or my fault. People grow away from each other. Spiritual growth is the law of life. Our obligation is to be true to ourselves and to relate to this law of life."

"Isn't marriage a relation?"

"Our marriage is a collapsed morality, like a burnt-out star which collapses into itself, gives no light and is heavy heavy heavy."

Collapsed morality. Law of life. More stately mansions. Here are unmistakable echoes of her friend Alistair Fuchs-Forbes. A few years ago Doris, who joined the Unity church, got in the habit of putting up English lecturers of various Oriental persuasions, Brahmin, Buddhist, Sikh, Zoroastrian. Two things Doris loved, the English people and Eastern religion. Put the two together, Alistair Fuchs-Forbes reciting *I Ching* in a B.B.C. accent, and poor Episcopal Doris, Apple Queen, from Winchester, Virginia, was a goner (Ibid., 66–7).

Doris is a "goner" because she has become hooked on other people's ideas—both poetic and spiritual—and has thereby lost both herself and the only one who really loves her. Tom has just asked her if she is "going to meet Alistair and the gang of fags." She replies:

> "Don't call him that. He's searching like me. And he's almost found peace. Underneath all that charm he's—
> "What charm?"
> "A very tragic person. But he's a searcher like me, a pilgrim."
> "Pilgrim my ass."
> "Did you know that for two years he took up a begging bowl and wandered the byways with a disciple of Ramakrishna, the greatest fakir of our time?"
> "He's a fakir all right. What he is is a fake Hindoo English fag son of a bitch." Why did I say the very thing that would send her away? (Ibid., 69)

In the midst of their last love-making one morning in the enclosed patio. Doris says to Tom:

> "You know the trouble with you, Tom?"
> "What?"
> "You don't understand a purely spiritual relationship."
> "That's true."
> Somewhere Doris had got the idea that love is spiritual (Ibid., 71).

Thus we see the not uncommon movement, into an essentially self-seeking spirituality as an escape from the boredom of life and the anxieties of freedom and responsible love. It is a movement into the ideas of others through books or persons in the hope that this is where real life is to be found. Clearly Doris is moving away from real life and into a self-destructive angelism as she leaves Tom for the two English homosexuals who are interested only in her money.

Tom says with wry irony as the marriage breaks up: "Here was where I had set a record: that of all cuckolds in history, I am the first American to be cuckolded by *two* English fruits."

Sutter Vaught

The final example of one who actively seeks his life in the world of abstraction is Dr. Sutter Vaught of *The Last*

Gentleman. Sutter is a complex person who cannot easily be categorized. However, it is clear that he is a highly abstracted person who progressively moves away from the nourishment of the concrete world and into solitary despair. The sub-plot of the story has to do with his decline and his final rescue from suicide.

Sutter is the kind of person who tends to actively think himself out of the world and into the realm of ideas, thereby, as he puts it in his notebook, slipping into "the orbit of transcendence." Finding himself there, he has extreme difficulty reentering the concrete world of persons and things. There is only one way in which he manages temporarily to accomplish the reentry and that is by sexual intercourse, not in a personal relationship but only as a "good pornographer." Unfortunately he continually finds this avenue to be self-defeating, as he opines again and again in his casebook.

> Man who falls victim to transcendence as the spirit of abstraction . . . , has no choice but to seek reentry into immanent world *qua* immanence. But since no avenue of reentry remains save genital and since reentry coterminus c̄ orgasm, post-orgasmic despair without remedy (*TLG*, 331).

The parallel to Kierkegaard's Faust, who used sexuality to assuage the despair arising from the same cause, is inescapable.

Sutter, however, is not immature, as his ex-wife, Rita, thinks. He is a tragic figure, struggling to find intellectual answers but increasingly moving away from human relationships that nourish life. He is both blessed and cursed with what Percy calls in *The Moviegoer* a "nose for the merde," something that all of Percy's heroes, and obviously Percy himself, share. That is to say, Sutter has a keen sense of human "paltriness" which he sees as the sum and substance of human sin today. He says that he chooses lewdness over paltriness. He sees himself as "the only sincere American" because he doesn't pretend to be a good family man while secretly engaging in extramarital sex.

> Soap opera is overtly decent and covertly lewd. The American theater is overtly lewd and covertly homosexual. I am overtly

> heterosexual and overtly lewd. I am therefore the only sincere American.
>
> Last night Lamar Thigpen called me un-American. That is a lie. I am more American than he is because I elect the lewdness which he practices covertly (Ibid., 281).

It is his honesty, his keen-eyed pricking of the bubble of human self-satisfaction and self-righteousness along with his willingness to travel a solitary road that constitute Sutter's appeal to Will Barrett. Will believes that Sutter is "onto something." He himself is searching for that one indispensable answer that would set his life in order, and he pursues Sutter through the story hoping to pry the answer from him.

The other side of Sutter, however, is his pride, arrogance, and superciliousness toward the human race in general. In his vision of the paltriness of people, he imagines himself to be in a superior state. His ideas about people are perceptive and damning, but his problem is that he lives primarily *in* his ideas and is thus abstracted from a personal relationship with whomever he may be with at any moment. This is his mode of *active* angelism.

Sutter is both so complex in the intermingling of his positive and negative qualities and so advanced in his angelism that a closer look will be undertaken in his case than in previous examples: It appears that by the end of *The Last Gentleman* Sutter has advanced in abstraction beyond Kierkegaard's Faust figure. Whereas the latter still hoped to find an answer in the realm of thought, Sutter toward the end has given up hope. Having found no answer, he has despaired and has, in Kierkegaard's words, gone "over to the camp of rebellion," affirming nihilism as his sole *raison d' etre* (*CD*, 122). He has come to the state that Kierkegaard calls the "demoniacal." In this condition he defiantly clutches his *un*freedom, as his one self-distinguishing value, and must repulse the possibility of freedom which could lead to the reintegration of himself.

Before proceeding to a closer look at the evidence from which the above conclusions are drawn, it may be helpful to place Sutter in the story. He is the older brother of Val, Kitty, and Jamie Vaught, with whose family Will Barrett has fallen into a relationship following a chance encounter in New York

City where Will is living. The Vaughts are from Will's part of Alabama and know his family. They are in New York seeking medical help for Jamie, aged 16, who has developed debilitating symptoms from an unknown cause. Will had met the Vaughts as the result of his having observed Kitty through his telescope in Central Park one day and having fallen in love with her at first sight. Friendship develops between Will and both Kitty and Jamie, and Mr. Vaught, senior, seizes the opportunity to ask Will to be a companion for the ailing Jamie for a year on their return to Alabama. Will agrees and follows the family south where he first meets the elder brother, Sutter.

In his father's words his oldest boy is a "failed physician." Mr. Vaught tells Will that Sutter had graduated from Harvard Medical School with the second highest grades ever made there. After interning he had returned home to Alabama, "practiced for four years with wonderful success. Was doing people a world of good. Then he quit" (*TLG*, 79). There is ample evidence to support the view that he quit primarily because he had begun to see through it all. Like the author of Ecclesiastes, he had begun to see that the things people usually strive for amount to nothing. Unfortunately, his keen vision into the dark side of life and his pride in his exalted vision prevented his moving to any kind of faith. Being an "Alabama Christian" certainly did not appeal to him.

The immediate episode that precipitated Sutter's quitting his practice indicates that he had been a perceptive, caring, and courageous doctor, though not a very politic one. He had ordered that a dying patient be taken out of his oxygen tent and allowed to go home to his family and garden where he could "die well" and not simply be "eased out," not knowing what was going on. The patient died, peacefully. The family sued for malpractice and the insurance company cancelled Sutter's insurance. He decided it was time to quit. He took his share of his inheritance, $100,000, and went West where he bought a small ranch.

Sutter at this point in the story appears as a person who has caring and creative instincts and yet is irresponsible. He wants to get away from it all where the concrete problems and relationships of the world will not bother him and where he may find the real thing in transcendence. He confides to his casebook:

> *Genius loci* of Western desert did not materialize. Had hoped for free-floating sense of geographical transcendence, that special dislocatedness and purity of the Southwest which attracted Doc Holliday and Robert Oppenheimer, one a concrete Valdosta man who had had a bellyful of the concrete, and the other the luckiest of all abstract men. . . . It didn't work (*TLG*, 335).

In a related entry he says: "But there transcendence failed me and Rita picked me up for the bum I was and clothed and fed me." As will become apparent, Sutter bears striking resemblance to the consumptive and death-dealing Doc Holliday of the American West. He married Rita, as he said later, "to stay alive," but the marriage did not work out. They were both victims of angelism. They "ate the pure fruit of transcendence," but neither could really see or know the other in his or her concrete reality. When Will comes upon Sutter in the Vaughts' home in Alabama the latter is divorced and working as assistant coroner and hospital pathologist. In the disappointed words of his father, he is a "thirty-four-year-old intern" (Ibid. 82).

The more detailed look at Sutter Vaught may well begin with the glimpse early in the story into his central concern. We find it in the title of an article that Sutter has written, a copy of which Jamie is reading as he lies in the hospital. It is

The Incidence of Post-orgasmic Suicide in Male University Graduate Students, divided into two sections:

"Genital Sexuality as the Sole Surviving Communication Channel between Transcending—Immanent Subjects," and

"The Failure of Coitus as a Mode of Reentry into the Sphere of Immanence from the Sphere of Transcendence." (Ibid., 62)

Will, we are told, "read the article twice and could not make head or tail of it." Sutter's casebook entries provide the best clue to what he sees to be the modern plight from which he himself suffers acutely. In an entry consisting of notes from an autopsy of a forty-nine-year-old white male found "rolled in a room above Mamie's . . ."

> Lewdness—sole concrete metaphysic of layman in age of science—sacrament of the dispossessed. Things, persons, relations emptied out, not by theory but by lay reading of theory . . . The latter is "real," the former is not (cf. Whitehead's displacement of the Real) (Ibid., 269).

Percy, through Sutter, is once again stating his recurring theme: we are seduced through a misunderstanding of science into seeing the expert's theory as more real than the actual person or thing in front of us, about which the expert is theorizing. Thus we find ourselves dispossessed of our own real world.

Later, alone in the Arizona desert, after reading one of Sutter's casebook entries, Will shivered: "What I need is my Bama bride and my cozy camper, a match struck and the butane lit and a friendly square of light cast upon the neighbor earth, and a hot cup of Luzianne between us and the desert cold, and a warm bed and there lie dreaming in one another's arms." (Ibid., 343) The contrast between Sutter in his abstracting orbit and Will with his warm Bama bride is crucial, in spite of the light tone in which it is described.

The essential barrenness of living in the intellectual sphere alone, divorced from the concrete wellsprings of bodily reality is symbolized by a geographic analogy. Percy contrasts the barrenness of the West with the plenitude of the South:

> [Will] sat down under the cistern and sniffed a handful of soil. The silence was disjunct. It ran concurrently with one and did not flow from the past. Each passing second was packaged in cottony silence. It had no antecedents. Here was three o'clock but it was not like three o'clock in Mississippi. In Mississippi it is always Wednesday afternoon, or perhaps Thursday. The country there is peopled, a handful of soil strikes a pang to the heart, *déjà vus* fly up like a shower of sparks. Even in the Southern wilderness there is ever the sense of someone close by, watching from the woods. Here one was not watched. There was no one. The silence hushed everything up, the small trees were separated by a geometry of silence. The sky was empty map

space. Yonder at Albuquerque forty miles away a mountain reared up like your hand in front of your face.

This is the locus of pure possibility, he thought, his neck prickling. What a man can be the next minute bears no relation to what he is or what he was the minute before (Ibid., 341–2).

We may note that it was always to the abstract West that Sutter gravitated in his attempt to find his "answer," his attempt somehow to deal with life, having found the concrete here-and-now not to his liking.

In the event that the reader, in trying to grasp Percy's meaning, finds he has "read it twice and could not make head or tail of it," one relatively more explicit casebook entry may help before proceeding:

> We are doomed to the transcendence of abstraction and I choose the only reentry into the world which remains to us. What is better than the beauty and the exaltation of the practice of transcendence (science and art) and of the delectation of immanence, the beauty and the exaltation of lewd love? What is better than this: one works hard during the day in the front line and with the comradeship of science and at night one goes to La Fonda, where one encounters a stranger, a handsome woman (Ibid., 339–40).

Science and art are in the orbit of transcendence; the woman is in the sphere of the immanent. She is flesh and blood, bodily, tangible and with her "the blood sings with voluptuousness and tenderness." Human relationship is bodily and placed, while relationship with the abstractions of science and art can take place anywhere and is only in the head. To exist wholly in abstraction is to be cut off from the "ordinary lovely world." As Percy says elsewhere: "Music is a whore."

Sutter's Nose for Merde
A predominant trait in Sutter, which gives primary impetus to his tendency to abstraction, is his keen awareness of human failing—"paltriness" to use his descriptive word. He truly has a "good nose for merde, for every species of shit that flies" (M, 228). His seeing so clearly the negative in persons drives him

to the realm of abstraction, Kierkegaard's "thought experiments," both as an easier way to spend his time and in an attempt to understand the human plight.

When readers are first introduced to Sutter they can see the basic charge he lays against humanity. Will, whose room in the Vaught home is next to Sutter's, hears a shot fired one evening. Will had been observing Sutter talking with his sister Val a few minutes before by peering into the next room, through a hole in his closet. He sees Val leave, and in a few minutes, having left his observation post, hears the shot. He lurches into Sutter's room.

> "Excuse me," said the reeling engineer. "I thought I heard a noise."
> "Yes."
> "It sounded like a shot."
> "Yes."
> He waited but Sutter said no more.
> "Did the pistol go off accidentally?"
> "No. I shot him."
> "Him?" The engineer suddenly feared to turn around (*TLG*, 207).

It turns out that Sutter had taken a shot at a picture on the wall of "The Old Arab Physician." Will notices that "the Arab who was ministering to some urchins with phials and flasks, was badly shot up."

Will asks "Why him?" and Sutter refers him to the poem, "Abou Ben Adhem," below the picture which, he says, compresses "the sum and total of all the meretricious bullshit of the Western World." In the poem Ben Adhem is commended by an angel for being ahead of everyone else in loving God because he loves his fellow men. Ben Adhem symbolizes to Sutter the contemporary Western world's exaltation of man and its forgetting of God, as well as what he sees as the Church's tacit concurrence with this "new gospel." (Ibid., 208)

Sutter's negative feelings, against both those who believe they can live without God and "Alabama Christians" who believe they have God in their pockets, come out periodically and strongly. In a casebook entry in which he carries on an imaginary conversation with his sister Val, a Roman Catholic nun, he says: "I could never accept the proposition . . . that I must spend eternity with Southern Baptists. But I understand what you did and even rejoiced in the scandal of it, for I do not in the least mind scandalizing the transcending scientific assholes of Berkeley and Cambridge and the artistic assholes of Taos and La Jolla." (Ibid., 295) His casebook entry continues a few lines later:

> The reason I am more religious than you and in fact the most religious person I know: because, like you, I turned my back on the bastards and went into the desert, but unlike you I didn't come sucking around them later.

> There is something you don't know. They are going to win without you. They are going to remake the world and go into space and they couldn't care less whether you and God approve and sprinkle holy water on them. They'll even let you sprinkle holy water on them and they'll even like you because they'll know it makes no difference any more. All you will succeed in doing is cancelling yourself. At least have the courage of your revolt (Ibid., 296).

A later entry again indicates his antipathy to conventional Christians:

> Christ should leave us. He is too much with us and I don't like his friends. We have no hope of recovering Christ until Christ leaves us. There is after all something worse than being God-forsaken. It is when God overstays his welcome and takes up with the wrong people (Ibid., 357).

Sutter's strongest negative feelings come out in what he sees of human failings in the god-relationship. He deplores the smugness of Western man whom he sees as vainly self-satisfied with his many achievements in science, industry, the arts, and philanthropy.

Sutter as Demoniac

Unfortunately, Sutter's keen negative vision of man is not matched by any countervailing hope. He gives up hope and thereby moves one critical step beyond Kierkegaard's Faust into a state of rebellion against the good which Kierkegaard calls "the demoniacal" state.

Kierkegaard defines the demoniacal as a state in which the person is "in dread of the good" (CD, 105). By this he means that the individual is in dread of possibility for his or her life and of the challenge to develop oneself. Every person experiences anxiety when confronted with some new possibility and freedom, but in the healthy person the dread arises out of a basic desire to advance or grow; it is thus, at bottom, a "dread of the evil." The person's dread then consists in a fear of what will prevent this actualization of self. It is a dread rooted in each person's awareness of his or her own vulnerability. In Kierkegaard's words, "It is dread in view of the reality of sin in view of the future possibility of sin." In the demoniacal state, on the other hand, the person has made an inner movement by which that person has gone "over to the camp of rebellion." Here the individual claims his or her own inability as the one mark of distinction to hold on to at all costs. Instead of dreading what will prevent growth the person dreads any challenge to grow. In cynicism the demoniac endeavors to shut out freedom, nor is this state restricted to extreme cases, for, as Kierkegaard points out, "a trace of this is to be found in every man, as sure as every man is a sinner." In whatever degree it may be present, however, it can be expressed in Kierkegaard's words: "Let me be the miserable man that I am." The first and central characteristic of the demoniacal state, then, is that it takes its self-imposed bondage to itself and affirms it as its one reason for being (CD, 101–22). "If we are no longer spiritually rich we forget God and take pride in being lost" (JH, 744).

An aspect of this central characteristic is the close reserve or "shut-upness" of the demoniacal person. Kierkegaard sums up the dual essence of the state when he says, "The demoniacal is unfreedom which would shut itself off." Again he says, "The demoniacal is *shut-upness unfreely revealed*." In contrast, "freedom is precisely expansive"; it "is constantly communicating" (CD, 110). Kierkegaard distinguishes the demoniacal from the reserve of the creative person. As he puts it, "one cannot be shut up in God or in the good, for this kind of reserve is precisely the utmost expansion." (Ibid., 119) Unfreedom however "becomes more and more shut up and wants no communication. The demoniacal person desires to remain mute; it is precisely his speaking, revealing his secret, which could save him.

Sutter appears as one who has elected to be a victim of unfreedom, or fate. He does so both in his words and in his general manner. His conversation is laced with expressions which reveal one who sees himself as no longer able to act creatively. For example, he seems acutely aware of the fact that he can no longer function in the normal manner of a physician. In the following exchange, which followed just after Sutter's disparagement of Abou Ben Adhem, he asks Will if he is going into a fugue.

> "I don't know. I thought perhaps that you—"
> "Me? Oh no. I haven't practiced medicine for years. I'm a pathologist. I study the lesions of the dead" (*TLG*, 209).

Sutter goes on to say that he cannot practice medicine because his liability insurance has been cancelled.

> "I'm not asking you to practice. I only want to know what you know."
> But Sutter only shrugged and turned back to the Colt. (Ibid.)

Thus, when approached by Will who asks for help to live, Sutter is threatened. In seeking his security in unfreedom he repulses anything that would take him out of it or even remind him of the possibility of freedom, or wholeness. He shuts it out. He shrugs and turns back to the symbol of the only fulfillment for which he seems to yearn: his own extinction.

Sutter's closed-in-ness is seen again a little later in the same encounter. He says to Will: "You are a very persistent young man. You ask a great many questions." "And I notice you don't answer them." Will then brings up a matter which touches upon the sexuality that Sutter, like Faust, employs to assuage his despair. Will has asked whether his own nervous condition could be caused by not having sex.

> "Sexual intimacy," said Sutter thoughtfully. He turned around suddenly. "Excuse me, but I still don't quite see why you single me out. Why not ask Rita or Val, for example? . . .
> "Well, I will not tell you," said Sutter after a moment.
> "Why not?"
> Sutter flushed angrily.

After repeating again with profanity that he will not tell Will, Sutter says,

> "Who do you think I am, for Christ's sake? I am no guru and I want no disciples. You've come to the wrong man." . . .
> Sutter turned away.
> "That's not why I came to you."
> "Why then?"
> "As a matter of fact, to ask what it is *you* cleave by."
> "Dear Jesus, Barrett, have a drink." (Ibid., 215–16)

With this, the first meeting between the two comes to a close. In his last statement Will has probed to the core of Sutter's secret. This secret, as we shall see more fully, is that he "cleaves by" the defiant assertion of his own misery and unfreedom and by the contemplation of his self-destruction. Sutter decisively shuts off further probing with his ' "Dear Jesus, Barrett, have a drink." '

Will and the reader meet Sutter the second time in the Vaughts' kitchenette a night or two later. The household has retired for the evening when Rita comes to Will's door to ask him to "settle a . . . point" between herself and her former husband. This occasion, along with a past incident alluded to in their conversation, further elucidates Sutter's way of living. First to be noted is the predominant element of apathy and self-isolation which, on both sides, marks the meeting between Sutter and Rita. They do not engage or really act with each other but merely play old tapes from the past. The bound state into which Sutter has allowed himself to fall is evident. The "closed expired air of impasse" impressed itself upon Will when he first entered the kitchenette. This atmosphere of impossibility, the sense that all is over, which so marks Sutter's bearing, permeates the conversation which takes place. The strong note of things being over, of the present being dead for Sutter and Rita, is felt by Will as he feels "their apathy steal into his bones." Sutter's expression is described as "fond and inattentive," where "fond" is understood in its meaning of "loss of feeling" under the influence of the "almost comfortable malice that is sustained between them." They quarrel "with the skillful absent-minded malice of married couples," not quite looking at each other but addressing each other "through the engineer." Sutter "could not tear his vacant eye" from Will, and Rita speaks "smiling but still unfocused." Thus with respect to each other they are not engaged in action that truly responds to the other but are vacant and absent from one another. Each with regard to the other is alone, focused on grievances of the past.

Sutter's closed-in state may be further indicated by the way in which he speaks to Will on another occasion:

> The engineer frowned. He felt a stirring of anger. There was something unpleasantly ironic about Sutter's wry rapid way of talking. It was easy to imagine him ten years from now haunting a barroom somewhere and pattering on like this to any stranger. He began to understand why others made a detour around him, so to speak, and let him alone (Ibid., 259).

Others let him alone simply because Sutter is not himself present with anyone. A wry, rapid way of talking implies neither a listener nor a speaker, but merely ideas being ground out by a machine. He does not put himself into his words and thereby reveal himself as a person speaking to another person. Thus he can indeed be imagined as a ghost haunting a barroom somewhere, "pattering on like this to any stranger." Patter characterizes the speech of con-men and comedians, and to be lost in the aesthetic mode is precisely to be a dealer in such illusion and lack of seriousness. No wonder Will felt a stirring of anger and others detoured around Sutter, because one is essentially ignored by such a person who lives in the immediacy of his own solipsistic thoughts.

Sutter gives the impression of being even more closed in upon himself when Will goes to him a few nights later for help against the onslaught of an attack of *déjà vu*. It was three o'clock in the morning and Will, seeing a light under Sutter's door, knocked. Sutter answered immediately.

> He was sitting in the wagonwheel chair, dressed in the same clothes, feet flat on the floor, arms lying symmetrically on the rests. There was no drink or book beside him.
>
> At last Sutter turned his head. "What can I do for you?" The naked ceiling bulb cast his eye sockets into bluish shadow. The engineer wondered if Sutter had taken a drug.

The hour, 3 A.M., the fact that he had not gone to bed as indicated by his wearing the same clothes as the night before, his unusual sitting posture, the fact that he has no drink or book beside him, and finally his haggard tone and appearance all point to a man in despair and self-absorption. "At last Sutter turned his head and said, 'What can I do for you?'" These words, the formal cliché of a shopkeeper to a stranger, convey in the present circumstance annoyance at being bothered. Sutter's orientation toward death is brought out in his response to Will's plea for help in his approaching fugue.

> "Jimmy is in there dying. Don't you think I should be more concerned with helping him?"
>
> "Yes, but I am going to live, and according to you that is harder." (Ibid., 260)

The seduction of death for the despairer is the easier way, as Will here suggests Sutter knows. Sutter's drift toward it is the non-action of aesthetic immediacy. In his close reserve he fends off Will's request to "tell me what you know." Without a smile Sutter answers, " 'Why do you ask me?' " and then dismisses Will's seriousness with, " 'Why don't you get married and live happily ever afterwards?' " Will becomes more insistent in his questioning but is repeatedly closed out.

Sutter's Death Wish
Sutter's suicidal tendencies have been mentioned in passing. In considering more specifically this extreme manifestation of

Sutter's shut-up-ness and his rebellion against the good, several specific bits of evidence will be considered. We have noted Sutter's fondness for his automatic pistol. His sister Val's remark when she saw him "aiming it here and there, laying the muzzle against his cheek" indicates her awareness of his tendency:

> "Put that thing up," said Val.
> "Why?"
> "Someday you're going to blow your fool head off—by accident."
> "That would offend you more than if I did it deliberately wouldn't it?"
> "And it would please you, wouldn't it, to die absurdly?" (Ibid., 206)

Sutter is aware that dying by accident is now more likely for him than deliberate suicide. He may be aware that as someone entrenched in the world of abstractions he is not likely to make such a final decision. On a prior occasion he had attempted suicide and failed. It was brought on by depression at the time of his first awareness of the nature of Jamie's illness. As his casebook reveals, the depression made him concupiscent. He invited a blond at the Mesa Motel pool up to her room. "Afterwards very low. Went to ranch, shot myself, missed brain, carried away cheek." The formula for all despair says Kierkegaard, is "in despair to will to be rid of oneself" (SD, 153).

Sutter's self-destructive tendencies come out often in less obvious ways. Just prior to his second trip West, when he took Jamie with him, a revealing incident took place at the hospital which resulted in his being dismissed:

> "Sutter," said Rita, warming her hands at the invisible embers and stamping her feet softly, "persuaded a ward nurse to leave her patients, some of whom were desperately ill, and accompany him to an unoccupied room, which I believe is called the terminal room. There they were discovered in bed by the night supervisor, and surrounded by pictures of a certain sort."

Rita goes on to point out to the others that Sutter's being discovered was "not simply bad luck." He had set the time for the rendezvous just a few minutes before the night supervisor made her rounds.

"Do you mean Sutter wanted to get caught, Ree?" cried Kitty.

"There are needs, my dear," said Rita dryly, "which take precedence over this or that value system." (Ibid., 264–5)

The fact that it was done in the terminal room, which he on prior occasions has known to be an antidote to despair, removes all doubt as to the need to which Rita refers. She knows the acuteness of his despair.

Kierkegaard provides a graphic example of a person who uses destruction to soothe the melancholy which results from repressing personal choice. This is the Roman emperor Nero. Kierkegaard depicts Nero as one who has been able to repress the voice of conscience and truth because of the diversions constantly available to him. But as his melancholy deepens he requires more radical diversions to ease it. He wreaks destruction on the world, burns Rome, and has innocent people killed in an attempt to surmount his despair.

> He is capable of having a child cut down before the mother's eyes to see if her despair would give passion a new expression which would entertain him. If he were not Emperor of Rome, he perhaps would end his life with suicide; for in truth it is only another expression for the selfsame thing when Caligula wishes that the heads of all men were set upon one neck so as to be able with one stroke to annihilate the whole world, and when a man puts himself to death (E/O II, 192).

Like Nero, Sutter must destroy in order to find relief. Since he is not the Emperor of Rome, with his power for destruction, he is like the one to whom Kierkegaard's Judge William points, who "may end his life with suicide."

It gradually becomes apparent that Sutter intends to take his life as soon as he has discharged his responsibility to his brother—that is, after Jamie's death. The first explicit hint of this comes out in his conversation with Will who has finally caught up with them in a small town in Arizona.

> "Where do you work?"
>
> "At a guest ranch," said Sutter absently. "It's something like being a ship's doctor. It's only temporary, until——" He shrugged (TLG, 347).

Sutter's state is revealed in an encounter with Will at the guest ranch, shortly before Jamie's death. Will finds him "sitting in the sheriff's chair on the front porch of Doc's cottage."

> "I remember everything now, Dr. Vaught," he said calmly, no longer agitated. "You said I was to come and find you. Very well, here I am. What was it you wished to tell me?" . . .
> Sutter sighed and sank into himself. (Ibid., 361)

Sutter, who had been sitting "slumped and unresponsive" to the dudes who smiled and nodded to him, didn't seem to hear Will. He only slumped further and gazed at the brown mountain.

> "Then you have nothing to tell me," the engineer asked him again.
> "That is correct. Nothing."
> "But, Sir, you wrote many things in—"
> "In the first place I didn't write them to you. In the second place I no longer believe a word of it."

It is Sutter's casebook that is referred to here. He goes on to quote Wittgenstein's saying, "Whereof one cannot speak thereof one should keep silent." Will asks him if he believes that, and he responds flatly, "No, I don't even believe that." Sutter's actions and his intention, which he states in a few moments, support his words that he no longer believes in anything. He again has his Colt Woodsman by his side and now sights it "at an airliner which sparkled like a diamond in the last of the sunlight" (Ibid.). He rambles on at length, ignoring Will's repeated attempts to engage him in consideration of his problem. He speaks disparagingly of Val who, he says, made the religious movement but then "sold out." He tells Will that when he first came to the desert he was waiting for a sign, "but there was no sign and I am not waiting for one now."

Finally Sutter allows his visitor to ask his question. It refers to Sutter's last casebook entry:

> I saw something clearly while I had no cheek and grinned like a skeleton. But I got well and forgot what it was. I won't miss next time (Ibid., 358).

Will wants to know what it was that he had discovered. Sutter continues to evade him, disavowing everything he had written in his casebook as "written to be rid of it, excreta, crap, and so intended." Finally Will presses him as to why he brought Jamie out West for the second time.

> Sutter shrugged.
> "But you brought him out. You must have hoped for something."
> "Only that he might get a little better."
> "Get better?" He watched the other like a hawk. "No, you mean die better, don't you?"
> Sutter shrugged and said nothing.
> "You didn't answer," said the engineer after a moment.
> Again Sutter's feet hit the floor. "Goddamn it, Barrett, what do you mean by requiring answers from me? Why should I answer you? What are you to me? Christ, if you recall I never solicited your company in the first place" (Ibid., 365–66).

As Will persists Sutter repeats three times that he will tell him nothing. Finally, he asks why his failure should be regarded as a badge of wisdom, and Will sees him for the first time as a man who has thrown himself away. He says to Will, "For both our sakes. Be done with me. Go stay with Jamie." Sutter's desire to seal himself off is thus evident. He is the "shut-up" despairer who, in Kierkegaard's words has "as it were, behind reality an enclosure, a world for itself locking all else out, a world where the despairing self is employed as tirelessly as Tantalus in willing to be itself" (SD, 207).

Finally, when Will suggests that he has an "enormous contribution to make, . . . Sutter rose so suddenly that the younger man was afraid he'd made him angry again" (TLG, 372). But he had only spotted one of the newly arrived female guests going into supper.

> Sutter rose creakily but cheerfully and rubbed his dry reedy hands together. "I do believe it is time to eat. Will you join me?"

A picture of what Kierkegaard calls "shut-upness" could not be more completely drawn. Sutter successfully encloses himself not only against Will's search for what he cleaves by, but also against any consideration of his own returning to the responsibilities and demands of life.

Sutter, however, is finally led to reveal his intention. This first opening of his closed-in state may have been instigated by his hearing from Will that his ex-wife, Rita, has gone away with another woman. Rita was the only person with whom Sutter had ever had any kind of relationship. She had been his salvation when he was down-and-out before, "and I married her to stay alive."

> "So Rita is gone." Sutter gazed into the empty sky, which instead of turning rosy with sunset was simply going out like a light."

He again picks up his Colt automatic.

> As the other watched him, Sutter began idly picking off dudes, sighting the Colt at one after another of the passing women, idly yet with a regardlessness which was alarming. It was a very small thing, no more than that Sutter did not take pains to conceal the pistol from the women, but for some reason the engineer's heart began to pound against his ribs.

His feelings as he aims his weapon recall words of Kierkegaard's:

> Perhaps there was someone who, reduced to the last extremity, only endeavored to concentrate his bitterness, his wrath, in a single passionate outburst, and sought vainly in the shrewdness which ordinarily understands life's emptiness and nothingness, until at last he burst forth: "Oh, the world and the lust thereof perish!" (ED II, 72).

Sutter's state of mind is further revealed by an incident he told "between shots" about a man,

> ". . . who was sitting with his family one Sunday evening watching Lassie, who had befriended a crippled duck and was protecting him from varmints. During the commercial he got up and got out his old army forty-five. When his family asked him what he intended to do, he told them he was going outside to shoot a varmint. So he went outside to the garage and got into the

family's second car, a Dodge Dart, and blew the top of his head off. Now that's a lot of damn foolishness, isn't it?" (*TLG*, 372).

Sutter, in his despair, longs to destroy the "varmint" of himself and all existence by putting "all heads on one neck," like Caligula, and pulling the trigger (*JH* I, 738). The same intention, and the disenchantment with life which lies behind it, had been indicated earlier in the conversation when he asked Will:

> "Which is the best course for a man: to live like a Swede, vote for the candidate of your choice, be a good fellow, healthy and generous, do a bit of science as if the world made sense, enjoy a beer and a good piece (not a bad life!). Or: to live as a Christian among Christians in Alabama? Or to die like an honest man?" (*TLG*, 364).

It is not until the end of the conversation that Sutter finally comes out with his secret. He had pointed out that someone would have to be there after Jamie dies. Will says:

> "I'll be here."
> "Some member of the family."
> "You'll be here."
> "No, Barrett, I'll not be here."
> "Why not?" asked the other angrily—he had had enough of Sutter's defections.
> "Barrett," said Sutter as cheerfully as ever, craning his neck to keep track of the new guest, "if you know anything at all— and, what with your peculiar gifts, you know a good deal more than that—you ought to know why not."
> "I don't," said the engineer, at a total loss. He had lost his intuition!
> "If I do outlive Jamie," said Sutter putting on his Curless jacket (double-breasted!), it will not be by more than two hours. What in Christ's name do you think I'm doing out here? Do you think I'm staying? Do you think I'm going back?" (Ibid., 373–4)

It has been necessary to probe at length in order to understand Sutter, because close reserve is worn like a garment precisely to prevent penetration to the inner secret. As Kierkegaard remarks, "There is no 'corresponding' mark, for in fact a corresponding outward expression corresponding to close reserve is a contradiction in terms" (SD, 206). Will had been attracted to Sutter as a significant figure who might help him. We have accompanied him in his gradual comprehension of this supposed guru.

It is clear that Sutter suffers from Kierkegaard's "sickness unto death." Not only his words, but his entire manner indicates a person who refuses to be engaged in life. Instead of interacting with others he attends only to his own thought-world. When Will goes to him with a problem it is like going to a doctor and being harangued with the doctor's pet peeves. His stance may be summed up in his own words: "I could have helped them once. I cannot do even that now. I am a pathologist" (TLG, 259). These words echo what Kierkegaard calls the most terrible line that could be put in a man's mouth: "At that time perhaps I might have been saved" (CD, 122). To *act* so as to "help them" is precisely the opposite of despair and may be the beginning of being saved: Sutter's closing out of Will has been repeatedly pointed out. He shrugs, sighs, slumps within himself, refuses to answer questions, changes the subject, and finally angrily cries, "What are you to me? Christ, if you recall I never solicited your company in the first place" (TLG, 366).

It is "revelation" alone says Kierkegaard that can cure the demoniac, and by revelation he means the demoniac's own revealing of his secret (CD, 113–15). Will is for Sutter the approach of "the good" in that he calls forth the eventual communication from the latter. What we have observed taking place between Will and Sutter in this respect is concisely delineated by Kierkegaard:

> The shut-up is precisely the mute; the spoken word is precisely the saving thing, that which delivers from the mute abstraction of the shut-up. Let the demoniacal here mean *x*; freedom's relation to it from without, *x*: the law for the revelation of the demoniacal is that against its will it comes out with it (CD, 111).

The revelation to be curative, however, depends on "whether he is willing to permeate that fact with freedom, assume the responsibility of it in freedom." This means that Sutter's gradual revelation of his problem to Will, and thereby to himself, can be curative, if he acknowledges that he is in this state by his own fault (CD, 107).

Sutter Vaught, then, is an unfortunate person who, by his own failure, finds himself having not only given up on life, but having also gone one dialectical step further. He clutches the despair of his unfreedom as a defiant protest against life itself. In his despair he moves toward his intended suicide through acts of symbolic and real destruction. That would be the ultimate destruction of one's world, and the ultimate rebellion against God (SD, 179). Sutter's is the extreme position of defiance and failure that is central to all refusal to act and be a responsible person in the world. As Kierkegaard points out, however, the demoniacal is never entirely in the power of evil and, as we have seen, Sutter has at least begun, albeit reluctantly, to come out of "shut-upness" in his coversations with Will. Consideration of the movement he apparently makes at the end of the book will be reserved for the final chapter.

Chapter 6

Kierkegaard's Injunction to Choose

If what has been described thus far were all that could be said about life we would have to agree that the human condition is problematic, to say the least. It would mean that people are dependent upon factors external to themselves, and thus are not sovereign actors. To live in "aesthetic immediacy" is to live like a puppet, without freedom. Is this the normal state for human beings? Both Kierkegaard and Percy utter a resounding "No!" to this question. What is the one thing by which one's life can be restored from the "death" of immediacy? Percy agrees with Kierkegaard that the one indispensable element is the act of personal choice. One must choose if one is to be. It is this act which literally constitutes the beginning of selfhood. Something new is born into the world when a person chooses to act on his own. Kierkegaard's Judge William says to the aesthetic young man in *Either/Or*, "You are not about to give birth to another human being; you are merely to give birth to yourself" (*E/O*, 210). He could not make his point much more emphatically than he does in his final work where he asserts that "Choice is the key to heaven" (*Attack*, 82).

The kind of choice that Kierkegaard means is a repeated choice, or inner decision to take charge of one's life. Such choice, as he sees it, is made possible by the experience of despair. Kierkegaard speaks of two fundamental kinds of choice in the movement to selfhood. The first takes a person out of aesthetic immediacy into the *beginnings* of responsible selfhood. This is the most crucial of the two because here one moves from passive dependency to becoming a deciding and acting person. It is thus essentially a movement from "death" into "life." However, the life into which one first moves cannot be sustained on its own. The individual finds that he or she cannot measure up to what life requires in its infinite demands for responsible action. In the despair occasioned by this fact one is enabled to make a second fundamental choice, "the second either/or," and that is the acceptance of the God-relationship.

What is involved in each leap to the next stage of existence is a letting go of what had previously given one's life meaning and support. This entails obvious risk, because one is not sure the new relationship can be achieved until the old is given up. The "leap" is like that of the trapeze artist: he must let go the support of the trapeze he is on in order to grasp the outstretched hands of his partner. The contemporary Roman Catholic theologian Gregory Baum describes what is involved:

> When Kierkegaard spoke of "the leap," he beautifully and powerfully announced an aspect of the Christian faith. The passage from the surface of reality to its depth is never a gradual process, a painless passage, supported by good arguments; it is rather a willingness to let go the superficial view, however scientific it may be, to negate it, and to be open in utter darkness to the deeper meaning of reality (*Comm*, 294).

CHOICE

Let us try to understand in more detail the crucial nature of human choice in Kierkegaard's view. Is it the content of the choice or the act itself that is important? How is genuine choice accomplished? Are we speaking of some crucial decision made once and for all, or is choice a continuing necessity for selfhood? These are among the questions that press for answers in Kierkegaard's thesis that "choice is the key to heaven." The wonder and beauty of choice is movingly expressed by Kierkegaard in the following:

> A choice! Do you, my hearer, know how in a single word to express anything which is more glorious? Do you know, even if you were to talk year in and year out, how you could mention anything more glorious than a choice, to possess the power of choice? For though no doubt it is true that the only blessed thing is to choose aright, yet the faculty of choice itself is truly the glorious prerequisite. What does it matter to the maiden to take note of all the prerequisite qualities of her future lord if she herself cannot choose? And, on the other hand, what more glorious thing does she know how to say than when, whether others praise the beloved's many perfections, or mention his many faults, she says: "He is my heart's choice!"? A choice! Yes, this is the jewel of great price, yet not intended to be buried and hidden away; for a choice which were not used is worse than nothing; it is a snare in which a man entangled himself as a slave, who did not become free—by choosing (CL, 64).

A true choice, then, works to create one's freedom, one's selfhood. By a choice one ceases to exist in hiddenness; he or she comes out and stands revealed. The young maiden in this prose poem proclaims her love, her innermost being, through her choice. Furthermore, she commits herself for the future by the choice in which she foregoes the possibility of choosing someone else. "The choice itself," says Kierkegaard, "is decisive for the content of the personality. Through the choice the personality immerses itself in the thing chosen; and when it does not choose, it withers away in consumption" (E/O II, 167). If someone puts off choosing until another has to choose for him, then he has, to that extent, lost himself. When this happens, one becomes "resolved into a multiplicity . . . and you thus would have lost the inmost and holiest thing of all in a man, the unifying power of personality." (Ibid., 164)

Of course, choosing must be a continuing and dynamic action if one is to maintain selfhood. "Existence," says Kierkegaard, "is the child that is born of the finite and the infinite, the eternal and the temporal, and is therefore a constant striving" (CUP, 85). His view of human existence is well expressed by the French philosopher Denis de Rougemont: "Between birth and death all man's reality is in his act."

Although Kierkegaard presents concrete occasions in which choice takes place, such as marriage and choice of vocation, he insists that it is the *act* of choice itself that is creative and not the particular thing that one chooses (*E/O* II, 180). Through Judge William he says that "in making a choice it is not so much a question of choosing the right as of the energy, the earnestness, the pathos with which one chooses." He insists, however, that choice of the kind that produces selfhood is at bottom always a choice between good and evil. What might appear to be a choice by a person essentially living in immediacy actually is not. In a life of immediacy one does not choose; he merely gravitates to the object of his desire of the moment. He may choose something entirely different in the next moment, thus no consolidating effect takes place in his personality. When, however, a person commits himself with "energy and pathos" in a choice for which he is prepared to assume responsibility in the future, then "the personality announces its inner infinity, and thereby, in turn, the personality is consolidated ... his nature is purified, and he himself brought into immediate relation to the external Power whose omnipresence interpenetrates the whole of existence" (Ibid., 170, 171).

Kierkegaard reaches his highest degree of eloquence in his writing on choice, in his conviction that literally everything depends upon it. His fictional ethicist, Judge William, says that he is "fighting for freedom ... for the future, for either/or" both in his writing and within himself. The Judge says that if he were on his death bed and his young son could thoroughly understand him, he would say to him:

> I leave to thee no fortune, no title and dignities, but I know where there lies buried a treasure which suffices to make thee richer than the whole world, and this treasure belongs to thee, and thou shalt not even express thanks to me for it lest thou take hurt to thine own soul by owing everything to another. This treasure is deposited in thine own inner self: there is an either/or which makes a man greater than the angels. (*E/O* II, 180)

The Judge continues, speaking poetically and with great beauty, about the inner experience of choosing:

> So when all has become still around one, as solemn as a starlit night, when the soul is alone in the whole world, then there appears before one, not a distinguished man, but the eternal Power itself. The heavens part, as it were, and the I chooses itself—or rather receives itself. Then has the soul beheld the loftiest sight that mortal eye can see and which never can be forgotten, then the personality receives the accolade of knighthood which ennobles it for an eternity. He does not become another man than he was before, but he becomes himself, consciousness is unified, and he is himself . . . ; for the great thing is not to be this or that but to be oneself, and this everyone can be if he wills it. (Ibid., 181)

He further asserts that the "experience of choosing imparts to a man's nature a solemnity, a quiet dignity which never is entirely lost."

Kierkegaard was careful to guard against any implication that what he saw as so essential for a person's acquisition of selfhood was in any way limited to those with certain gifts of insight or certain privileges of circumstance. The task of selfhood is one that is laid upon every person; this he emphasizes repeatedly throughout his works. For example, speaking of Socrates, he said that the latter as a "gadfly" wanted only to have ethical significance, rather than to be considered a genius, "because then they could say, 'It's all fine for him; he is a genius.' No, he only did what every man can do, he only understood what every man can understand" (JD, 577). It was Kierkegaard's mission to bring to every man, to the "serving maid" to whom he often referred, the need to act for his or her own self. In the sphere of religion, he said, one should not speak of special gifts, "for here the 'gift' is simply to will" and the man who does not will we ought to hold at least in sufficient respect not to pity him (for his lack of gifts)" (CD, 102). Everything is always brought back to the individual both by Kierkegaard and by Socrates, "for that is where the battle must be fought" (JD, 313).

The Essential Choice

We have seen Kierkegaard's insistence that choice as such is the key to acquiring one's self. There is, however, one *essential* choice without which the leap to a new level of existence cannot begin or continue. This is the willingness to accept one's own condition of despair.

This obviously requires some explanation, because a natural response might be "What despair? I am not despairing." Kierkegaard's answer to that would be that the one who so responds has so successfully covered up his despair that he does not feel it. Percy's epigraph to his first novel, *The Moviegoer*, is from Kierkegaard's *Sickness Unto Death:* ". . . the specific character of despair is precisely this: it is unaware of being despair."

Despair is the sense of dread that catches a person unaware at times, the sense of futility as he looks at his own life or as he sees his own failures and those of others, as he experiences the "hollowness" of the human condition, to use T.S. Eliot's term. Religious experience indicates that man is, in fact, hollow and utterly dependent upon God. "Choose despair" simply means: acknowledge your actual state. Only then can one begin to live in a healthy relationship to reality. Only then can one be at peace with oneself and out of the useless striving to do the impossible: to achieve some value of one's own, apart from God. A human says Kierkegaard, is neither a beast nor an angel, but a wayfarer on the move to the only relationship that can enable the individual to live: the relationship to God. Anxiety, dread, despair is the natural state of the person who has not made the inner movement into that relationship. The human being implicitly knows his own hollowness but attempts to deny it, to forget it, and to live on the basis of an imagined self-sufficiency. One cannot make this work over the long haul. His underlying awareness of his own hollowness is his despair.

Kierkegaard, then, says the first and continuing thing that one must do is to accept this condition; otherwise the person cannot begin to move to self-recovery. By choosing to stop the diversions of pleasure-seeking, busyness and self aggrandizement, he will be able to experience what in fact he is and thereby leap to what alone can sustain him.

"What then must you do?" says Judge William to his young aesthetic friend, as he finally comes to the nub of the question. He points out that some might say, "Get married" or "look for a job, throw yourself into the life of affairs" and you will have something else to think about; you will forget your melancholy, and you will find how your life is to be lived (*E/O* II, 211–12). The Judge cautions his friend that it is an open question as to whether this will help and reminds him that, in any case, it is beneath his professed ideals of chivalry to choose either a wife or a job merely to take care of his own needs. He points out that although he may momentarily repress his underlying despair, "occasionally it will break out and will be more dreadful than ever." To marry or get a job for these reasons alone is merely an aesthetic choice for immediate gratification, but this is exactly what he must leave behind if he is to become a self. There is, then, only one remedy that goes to the root of the problem, says the Judge: "What then must you do? I have only one answer: despair." He holds out this choice as a "deed which requires all the power and seriousness and concentration of the soul." (Ibid.)

When one chooses to acknowledge his or her despair, this inner shift establishes what T.H. Croxall called a "character *indelibilis*" which is not lost. "This is only the first step. . . . Yet having taken the first step, you cannot come back" (*E/O* II, 279).

It is possible to put off indefinitely coming to terms with one's own fundamental lack, but the longer one waits the more difficult the task becomes. The necessity never ceases, however, if one is to win the prize of selfhood. Judge William says to the young aesthete to whom he writes:

> I shout this to you, like the woman who offered to sell to Tarquin a collection of books and when he would not give the sum she demanded burned one-third of them and demanded the same sum, and when again he would not give the sum she demanded burned another third of them and demanded the

same sum until finally he gave the original sum for the last third (Ibid., 213).

The price of selfhood is the same, whether one pays it early in life or waits until only a third of life remains. The price, writes John Wild, is one's willingness to let go the apparent security of aesthetic diversions and to accept the awareness of one's true condition, so that he or she may move to the relationship that can sustain the self (*KCEP*, 34).

Anyone really hearing what Kierkegaard is urging in his insistence upon choosing despair would surely wonder just how one goes about doing this. Fortunately, one learns from Kierkegaard that one does not simply have to resolve to do it one bright morning and then proceed. The individual is not left on his own in that way. Kierkegaard asserts that specific occasions arise in everyone's life—which may be thought of as occasions of God's grace itself—in which this crucial life-choice may be accomplished. "There will come a moment in his life when his spirit will be ripened by the instant of choice" (*E/O* II, 221). Life will present these occasions, often in rather forceful ways: "the circumstances of your life may tighten upon you the screws in its rack and compel you to freedom." Again speaking through Judge William, Kierkegaard offers a striking example from his own life of how circumstances enabled his choice of despair and thence selfhood:

> It is on beautiful terms despair is offered to you, and yet there are more beautiful terms. Imagine a young man as talented as you are. Let him love a girl, love her as dearly as himself. Let him once ponder in a quiet hour upon what it is he has constructed his life and upon what she can construct hers. Love they have in common, and yet he will feel that there are differences. She possesses, perhaps, the gift of beauty, but this has no importance for him, and after all it is so fragile; she has perhaps the joyful temper of youth, but that joy has no great significance for him, but he possesses the power of the mind and feels the might of it. He desires to love her in truth, and it never occurs to him to attribute this power to her, and her meek soul does not demand it, and yet there is a difference, and he will feel that this must be done away if he is to love her in truth. Then he will let his soul sink into despair. It is not for his own sake

> he despairs but for hers, and yet it is for his own sake, too, for he loves her as dearly as himself. Then will despair devour everything till he finds *himself* in his eternal validity, but then he has also found her, and no knight can return more happily and gladly from the most perilous adventure than does he from this fight from flesh and blood and the vain differences of the finite, for he who despairs finds the eternal man, and in that we are all equal (Ibid., 213–14).

His essential choice and act is to "let his soul sink into despair," and out of this comes his movement to what can give him life in place of emptiness: he finds *himself* in his relationship to the eternal. His sense of dread had come from his grave doubts about his impending marriage, doubts about his rightness for Regine and her rightness for him. He could have smothered these doubts and married her, or he could have taken the difficult step of calling off the engagement. Neither of these can he bring himself to do. His despair intensifies. His creative act is to not run away from the despair, either through escape into forgetfulness through alcohol or other diversions, or through plunging into marriage. He turns his back on both of these escape routes and accepts the feelings of loss that ensue. This acceptance, after a time, has the effect of opening him to a new awareness . . ."he who despairs finds the eternal man." The psychiatrist Rollo May describes the role of anxiety in Kierkegaard's thought: . . ."accepting the human situation frankly, facing the fact of death and other aspects of the contingency of existence, and from this *angst der kreatur* one learns to interpret the reality of one's situation." (*MA*, 44)

Kierkegaard describes despair as the "indispensable third factor" which does more than merely disturb a person to act on his own. When one does not avoid despair, it goes further and "unlocks the hidden energies of [man's] spirit and affords him the opportunity to form those ideal resolutions of the will in which the life of the spirit is realized." (*KP*, 120) He describes it as "what the movement is in the clock; it is the movement in the Christian life" (*JD*, 262). Kierkegaard asserts the hopeful proposition that the sense of despair, of a gap, or of being lost will continue to afflict each individual, unless the person is forever successful in repressing it, until he or she finally accepts it and thereby makes the crucial movement into selfhood.

Finally we may particularly note that it is *intensification* of despair which provides the occasion for the crucial choice: It "must produce the necessary adequate fear":

> It is true of all edification that it must first and foremost produce the necessary adequate fear, for otherwise the edification is reduced to an illusion. The ethicist had with the passion of the infinite in the moment of despair chosen himself out of the fearful plight of having his self, his life, his reality in aesthetic dreams, in melancholy, in concealment (*CUP*, 231).

Kierkegaard maintains the enabling power of despair can almost compel one to act:

> However surprising it may seem, one may say therefore that only fear and trembling and only constraint can help a man to freedom. For fear and trembling and constraint can master him in such a way that it is not a question of any choice—and then one very likely chooses the right thing (*JH*, 1261).

He remarks elsewhere with irony and humor that "of course, many succumb during the cure, but it is also useful for a man to be handled as roughly as all that" (*JD*, 1158).

Everything depends upon how the individual responds when moments in life similar to those described come upon one. The many diversions available enable one to avoid dealing with despair. This, says Kierkegaard, was the case with the emperor Nero, who was continually able to divert himself with such pleasures as putting people to death and burning Rome. "His life demands a metamorphosis"—

> . . . it demands a higher form of existence. But if this is to come about, an instant will arrive when the splendor of the throne, his might and power, will pale; and for this he has not the courage. Then he grasps after pleasure (*E/O* II, 190).

Nero responds to his increasing despair by running after whatever can conceal it, and in so doing he remains a non-person.

Choosing One's Self

From what has been said about choosing despair, it is clear that what one accepts in this act, and thereby in effect creates, is one's own self. "And when a man despairs, he chooses again—and what is it he chooses? He chooses himself, not in his immediacy, not as this fortuitous individual, but he chooses himself in his eternal validity" (*E/O* II, 215). John Wild, in discussing Kierkegaard's understanding of *angst*, said the source of this feeling is "my own real possibilities looming up before me, my total being-in-the-world as it *might-be*, if I really become what I am." (*KC*, 34) Thus when a person accepts his *angst* he makes possible the becoming of the self as he is intended to be. That this is central to Percy's understanding of man is clear. He says, "The anxiety may be quite the reverse of a symptom. It may be the call of the self to the self" (*Amer*, 393). Kierkegaard states it unmistakably when he says through Judge William, ". . . to despair truly, one must truly will it, but when one truly wills it one is truly beyond despair; when one has truly willed despair one has truly chosen that which despair chooses, i.e., oneself in one's eternal validity" (*E/O* II, 217). One can grasp something of what this elusive self is by realizing that, though a person would perhaps like to have someone else's intelligence, or good looks, or wealth, one "never seriously expresses the wish that he might become another man." Kierkegaard refers to his self as "my other" which, in aesthetic immediacy," is suspended . . . it is a nothing vaguely hinted at" (*CD*, 38). Whereas, when I choose to accept my awareness of dread I am moved to a new condition: "In despair I choose the absolute" for I myself am the absolute" (*E/O* II, 217).

There is another important element in Kierkegaard's understanding of the act of choosing one's self; that is the element of repentance. He says, "I cannot often enough repeat the proposition, however simple it may be in itself, that choosing oneself is identical with repenting oneself. For upon this everything turns" (*E/O* II, 252-3). What does he mean by this? Does he mean simply that the action of choosing oneself involves acknowledging the guilt due to one's failures? He does mean this, but he means more. He means that to choose one's self means to accept what one has become by the choices he has made or failed to make.

> He is the man he is only in consequence of this history. Therefore, it requires courage for a man to choose himself; for at the very time when it seems that he isolates himself most thoroughly he is most thoroughly absorbed in the root by which he is connected with the whole. This alarms him, and yet so it must be, for when the passion of freedom is aroused in him (and it is aroused by the choice as also it is presupposed in the choice) he chooses himself and fights for the possession of this object as he would for his eternal blessedness; and it is his eternal blessedness. He cannot relinquish anything in this whole, not the most painful, not the hardest to bear, and yet the expression for this fight, for this acquisition is . . . repentance (Ibid., 220).

Repentance means acknowledgment of what one is and being sorry for what one's failures have made one. And yet having reached this point, the person is able to take up the battle for himself with joy. He has begun to sense himself in his "eternal validity."

> The individual thus becomes conscious of himself as this definite individual, with these talents, these dispositions, these instincts, these passions, influenced by these definite surroundings, as this definite product of a definite environment. But being conscious of himself in this way, he assumes responsibility for this (Ibid., 255).

Kierkegaard goes on to say that in order really to accept one's self one must also acknowledge and be sorry for the deprivation that the sins of his fathers have visited upon him. His own father's strict piety had had a crippling effect on Kierkegaard. In the moving passage that follows in *Either/Or* he says:

> For when I see my small son running about the room so joyful, so happy, I then think, "Who knows if after all I have not had an injurious influence upon him? God knows I take all possible care of him, but this thought does not tranquilize me." Then I say to myself, "There will come a moment in his life when his spirit will be ripened by the instant of choice, then he will choose himself, then also he will repent what guilt of mine may

rest upon him. And it is a beautiful thing for a son to repent his father's fault, and yet he will not do this for my sake but because he only thus can choose himself (Ibid., 221).

Choosing one's self, then, involves accepting the losses with which one has been afflicted. This is yet another aspect of choosing despair, with its effect of moving one to a new relationship to oneself. The world will again "become beautiful to you and joyful, although you see it with different eyes than before, and your liberated spirit will soar up into the world of freedom." (Ibid., 222)

Choice then, in Kierkegaard's perception, is the key to selfhood. Fundamentally necessary is the choice or acceptance of one's actual state, as a being who is not intended to make it on his own. One's sense of despair and fear of loss is what can enable the person to accept his or her true condition. When he is willing so to accept, when he chooses to, then he can move to a recovery of himself before God.

Walker Percy has acknowledged that his fictional heroes portray the kind of choice and action that Kierkegaard insists is essential to becoming a self. We turn now to consider some of these characters to see what "the movements" may look like in our times.

Chapter 7

Percy's Heroes Make the Choice

In Walker Percy's understanding of the crucial movement out of an immediate and passive relationship to things, ideas, and people, into the ability to act on one's own, the one thing absolutely necessary is the act of choice. He is in full agreement with Kierkegaard here. He adds a new insight of his own, however, based on contemporary philosophical understanding of human nature: To the process of self-becoming Percy gives a central role to the uniquely human act of symbolization. There is wide agreement among philosophers today that the human individual transcends his or her environment precisely in the act by which the person names or symbolizes things within it. Until one does this one is essentially only another organism within the environment, responding reflexively to it. When one symbolizes things within the environment he transcends it and becomes lord over it. That is, he becomes a self.

Thus, it can be said that when a young child begins to hear the names of things and to use these names himself the child ceases being merely an organism and becomes a person. However, in his central concern, which he shares with Kierkegaard and the existentialists in general, Percy insists that this ability must continually be recovered. Persons tend to lapse away from autonomous seeing and symbolizing and to fall back into dependency upon the worn clichés of the crowd.

The question then arises: how can one make the movement back to selfhood when one has fallen into this kind of dependent living which Kierkegaard terms "intellectual immediacy"? As Percy sees it, the factor enabling such a move is catastrophe or ordeal which comes upon one. What the *person* must do in the process, however, is to choose to accept the catastrophe or ordeal that is laid upon him. If he does so he can be enabled to break with immediacy and once again see, symbolize, and thereby act on his own.

Thus Percy is in full agreement with Kierkegaard's fervent and repeated injunction to "choose despair." Accepting catastrophe or ordeal and choosing despair mean essentially the same thing. If one makes this choice, something remarkable happens. One's bondage to the many pre-formed symbolic complexes in which one rests is broken and one becomes once again a sovereign, seeing, and acting self. One has moved into what Kierkegaard calls the ethical mode of existence in which for the first time one is responsible for what one does.

Percy portrays this movement to autonomous selfhood in his protagonists as it takes place in varied and complex ways. His philosophical essays cast light on what is going on in his fiction, and we shall continue to draw on this source as needed for clarification.

BINX

We return now for another look at Binx Bolling, Percy's first protagonist, this time to see how he makes the break that leads to the acquiring of self. Although the process is not completed in one isolated action, there is an initial act after which he seems to be a different person. His fiancée, Kate, refers to it as his "secret" and cites a similar secret of her own, which "gave me my life" (*M*, 58). As several literary critics have observed, Binx and Kate seem to be the only two alive persons in the story. The high significance of the event in question is made clear when Binx describes it as the occasion when he first became aware of "the possibility of a search." It occurred while he was serving as an infantry lieutenant in Korea:

> I remember the first time the search occured to me. I came to myself under a chindolea bush. Everything is upside-down for me, as I shall explain later. What are generally considered to be the best times are for me the worst times, and that worst of times was one of the best. My shoulder didn't hurt but it was pressed hard against the ground as if somebody sat on me. Six inches from my nose a dung beetle was scratching around under the leaves. As I watched, there awoke in me an immense curiosity. I was onto something. I vowed that if I ever got out of this fix, I would pursue the search (M, 10, 11).

The essential element of catastrophe is obviously present here: Binx is lying wounded. He does not fight it or rail against it. There he is; he accepts it. And then something happens: his interest is caught by a dung beetle scratching around among the leaves. He *sees* it as he has not seen things before, as a kind of "revelation of being."

Percy sets forth the same phenomenon in an article discussing the concerns of the religious novelist, that is "the novelist who is concerned with the radical questions of man's identity, his relation to God or to God's absence" (MB, 108). He describes the kind of character and event that such a novelist is interested in: A businessman commuting to work on the train suffers a severe heart attack—

> When he regains consciousness, he finds himself in a strange hospital surrounded by strangers. As he tries to recall what has happened, he catches sight of his own hand on the counterpane. It is as if he had never seen it before: he is astounded by its complexity, its functional beauty. He turns it this way and that. What has happened? Certainly a kind of natural revelation . . . which can only be called a revelation of being. . . . Is it not reasonable to say that in some sense or other the stricken commuter has "come to himself"? In what sense he has come to himself, how it transforms his relationship with his family, his business, his church, is of course the burden of the novel. (Ibid., 109)

Percy comments later in the same article that "when the novelist writes of a man 'coming to himself' through some such catalyst as catastrophe or ordeal he may be offering obscure testimony to a gross disorder of consciousness and to the need of recovering oneself as neither angel nor organism but as a wayfaring creature somewhere between." As we have previously noted, in Percy's terminology to be an "angel" or to be an "organism" is to exist in intellectual or in sensuous immediacy. In both of these instances of catastrophe the person is being enabled to perform an act of symbolization. Let us pause for a closer look at what Percy has to say about symbolization in his essays on the subject.

Symbolization in its most elementary form is the act of naming, but it includes the whole range of the uniquely human actions to acquire and use language and conceptual thought. Linguistic philosophers assert that it is through this act that one is related, as human, to the persons and things around him. Conversely, a person's alienation from the world, from others, and from himself is related to a failure of this process. As Percy explains it, "a symbol is the vehicle for the conception of an object" (*MB*, 280). If a person does not have a name for a thing, he cannot know it. To "know" in this case denominates "the existential sense of identification of the knower with the object known."

The continuing problem is that the symbol for something, when it becomes too familiar, can get in the way of seeing.

> The symbol "sparrow" is, at first, the means by which a creature is known and affirmed and by which you and I become its co-celebrants. Later, however, the same symbol may serve to conceal the creature until it finally becomes invisible. A sparrow becomes invisible in ordinary life because it disappears into its symbol. If one sees a movement in a tree and recognizes it and says it is "only a sparrow," one is disposing of the creature through its symbolic formulation. *Being is illusive; it tends to escape, leaving only a simulacrum of symbol. Only under the condition of ordeal may I recover the sparrow.* If I am lying wounded or in prison and a sparrow builds his nest at my window, then I may see the sparrow (*Pers*, 154, emphasis added).

What is involved, then, is the crucial act of seeing and naming which, when it is hindered or lost through over-familiarity can be enabled by a kind of grace in the form of some shock, catastrophe, or ordeal.

The act of symbolizing, he continues, can best be understood by means of a concrete example. Percy asks us to imagine a father telling his two-year-old son that this, pointing to a certain object, is a ball. At first the child thinks that the word "ball" only means for him to *do* something: run and get the ball. But then one day the father says "ball" and suddenly the son understands that "this *is* a ball—the word 'ball' *means* this round thing." Something fundamental has happened, says Percy, and "what has happened is nothing less than the discovery of the world and the coming to oneself as a person." (Ibid., 149)

In Percy's view something "without precedent in natural history" has taken place. "In nature there is cause and effect, and in subhuman animal nature there is, at the most, conditioned response . . ."

> The state following a nuclear fusion is, thus, a function of the state before. A dog's response to the signal "ball" is a function of the stimulus and the electrocolloidal state of the dog's brain. But when one names a thing or understands from another that a thing is so named, the event can no longer be interpreted as a causal function. (Ibid., 151)

What takes place in naming is the free act of "affirmation": "Naming or symbolization may be defined as the affirmation of the thing as being what it is under the auspices of the symbol." Percy cites Helen Keller's surprise and joy at first being able to do this when she realized that this wet substance "*is* water."

Naming things, says Percy, brings about a new orientation to the world which "is no longer biological; it is ontological."

> Prior to naming things, the individual is an organism responding to his environment; he is never more or less than what he is; he either flourishes or he does not flourish. A tiger is a tiger, no more, no less, whether he is a sick tiger or a flourishing tiger. But as soon as an individual becomes a name-giver or a hearer of a name, he no longer coincides with what he is biologically.

Henceforth he must exist either authentically or inauthentically. (Ibid., 153)

After he has "come to himself" as a sovereign see-er and namer, a person is aware of himself; he is an acting agent and, as such, responsible. He has moved into Kierkegaard's ethical stage.

For Binx lying wounded in the ditch, "the dung beetle is recovered for him" as he accepts what has happened. Suddenly he can see afresh. What he has recovered is himself as a "being in the universe (who) stands apart from the universe and affirms some other being to be what it is" (For, 7). He "experiences himself as the active bearer of his own powers and richness and not as an impoverished thing" (Amer, 416).

When one has thus recovered himself, what will he do? It is Percy's view that in one form or another he will begin a search for an answer to the question of who he is, where he came from, and where he is going. His activity is like that of the child who has learned that "this is a ball" and then wants to know what the other things are that he sees around him. When Binx saw the dung beetle, there awoke in him the possibility of the search. Gabriel Marcel, the contemporary French existentialist also describes this need to search when one has become aware:

> When I awake to myself, I note that I am situated or thrown into a world within which I have to find my orientation. Won't I suceed in discovering what this is by *exploring* this world, by determining why it is that I should find myself in this peculiar situation and what it implies both to the whole and to myself? . . . Finding myself in an indeterminate possibility in the situation in which I am placed, I must seek *Being* in the strict sense, if I am to find myself (CF, 223–4).

It may be argued that anything like what Percy describes in Binx's coming to himself in a ditch in Korea and being enabled to see afresh is a rather unlikely possibility for most people. Percy uses it, however, merely to provide a striking example of what normally takes place in more subtle ways. Percy once quoted Flannery O'Connor as saying: "for the near-blind you have to draw very large, simple caricatures" (MB, 118).

Will Again

Each of Percy's protagonists is enabled by a specific event of grace to perform the action of "choosing despair" and breaking through to heightened awareness. In his latest novel, *The Second Coming*, the hero is the middle-aged, early-retired Will Barrett, the same Will who was the young protagonist of the earlier novel, *The Last Gentleman*. As the young Will he was depicted making the movement to selfhood through the catalyst of catastrophe, and thereafter pursuing a passionate quest which culminated in a second breakthrough. In the later novel, Will as a middle-aged man is again struggling for his identity, which only shows that selfhood is never possessed once and for all but must be reacquired constantly.

When we meet Will in *The Second Coming* we see a man who seems to "have it all" in terms of social position, friends, and material benefits. He had retired three years before, at age forty-eight, from active partnership in a prestigious Wall Street law firm. He had returned with his wife, Marion, to live comfortably in the community in which he had grown up in North Carolina. Marion was a New York native of considerable independent wealth and an invalid. After settling into retirement she became quite active both in her Episcopal parish and in various charitable good works. Will supported her in these activities, taking her where she needed to go, carrying her from car to wheel chair and, in general, sharing marital companionship with her. His chief recreation was golf, which he played with a regular foursome made up of several local business and professional men. Three years after their return to North Carolina Marion died. Will continued, though somewhat less actively, in the charitable works she had begun.

The reader who is acquainted with Percy's work will not be surprised to find in the very first lines of the book that all is not well with Will Barrett, in spite of every outward appearance of his living the good life.

> The first sign that something had gone wrong manifested itself while he was playing golf.
> Or rather it was the first time he admitted to himself that something might be wrong.

> For some time he had been feeling depressed without know-ing why. In fact, he didn't even realize he was depressed. Rather was it the world and life around him which seemed to grow more senseless and farcicial with each passing day. . . . Once he fell down in a bunker. . . . More than once he shook his head and, smiling ironically, said to himself: This is not for me.
>
> Then it was that it occurred to him that he might shoot himself.
>
> First, it was only a thought that popped into his head.
>
> Next, it was an idea which he entertained ironically.
>
> Finally, it was a course of action which he took seriously and decided to carry out (*SC*, 3–4).

Percy's central concern as a thinker and author is revealed here. A man who has been going through life, seeming to do well, even to be highly successful, begins to be aware that something is wrong. Something happens, whether some ob-vious catastrophe, some intensification of boredom, some momentous decision, to make him aware of unease, of the abyss below him, of the "despair," to use Kierkegaard's term, that he has until now successfully concealed from himself. In this moment of intensification of despair he *may* begin to see afresh and recover himself.

How similar to Binx in the ditch is Will, suddenly finding himself lying flat on the ground in the bunker. And like Binx he is surprised to notice that "lying there, cheek pressed against the earth, he noticed that things looked different from this unaccustomed position. A strange bird flew past. A cumu-lus cloud went towering thousands of feet into the air. Ordin-arily he would not have given the cloud a second glance."

Does Will's recovery of himself consist merely in this falling and this new seeing? Yes and no. The present "catastrophe" may enable it, but in any case, this will be only the beginning of a process which goes on through the course of the narrative. In this novel the complexity of the movement is spelled out as well as its difficulty. It is one that in Percy's view too few peo-ple are willing to make: "How did they manage to deceive themselves and even appear to live normally, work as usual, play golf, tell jokes, argue politics? Was he crazy or was it rather that other people went to great lengths to disguise from themselves the fact that their lives were farcical? He couldn't decide." (Ibid., 3, 4)

As we read further we see that the occasion of Will's falling on the golf course is only the first such happening among a number. His "good buddy" golfing companions pretend not to notice or make much of it in their kindness or in their hesitancy to get too close to reality. Will's temptation to suicide continues and intensifies:

> Once again he found himself in the pretty reds and yellows of the countryside. As he drove along a gorge, he suffered another spell. Again the brilliant sunlight grew dim. Light seemed to rise from the gorge. He slowed, turned on the radio, and tried to tune in a nonreligious program. He could not find one. In the corner of his eye a dark bird flew through the woods, keeping pace with him. He knew what to do.
> Pulling off at an overlook, he took the Luger from the glove compartment of the Mercedes (Ibid., 13).

Will has done all the right things, had a meaningful and useful career, been faithful to his invalid wife to the end, given to charities, and so forth, but he has not accomplished the one essential task that Kierkegaard sees laid upon every person: he has not yet acquired his own self.

> There at any rate stands Will Barrett on the edge of a gorge in old Carolina, a talented agreeable wealthy man living in as pleasant an environment as one can imagine and yet who is thinking of putting a bullet in his brain. (Ibid., 14)

What is one to do to accomplish the task of becoming himself? Percy agrees with Kierkegaard that the one action which is necessary to begin upon it is to "choose despair." As we shall see more clearly in what follows, Will has already begun to perform this essential act; otherwise he would still be diverting himself with his fellows, cracking jokes, instead of standing alone in the rough off the fairway, listening and waiting. What Will must do, more specifically, in the action of choosing despair is to be willing to face and deal with the thing that he was reminded of on the first occasion of his blacking out on the golf course, ". . . the most important event in his life, yet he had managed to forget it." It is this event that Will is given the opportunity to name by means of the sickness that fells him from time to time. By this he can break from the clichés and jokes of his golf foursome and begin to see on his own.

What, then, is the one creative thing that Will must do to make this possible? He must choose to not evade any longer the thing he had for so long managed to forget: the time when he was twelve years old that his father had tried to kill him and himself when they were out hunting. Now, with his depression deepening, Will is called to pay attention to these old memories. He performs Kierkegaard's crucial action of choosing despair, of choosing not to evade the memories but to let them sink in and do their work.

> Now he stood alone in the glade after slicing out-of-bounds on eighteen. He was holding the three-iron, not like a golf club or a shot gun now, but like a walking stick. . . .
>
> Once he was in the pine forest the air changed. Silence pressed in like soft hands clapped over his ears. Not merely faint but gone, blotted out, were the shouts of the golfers, the clink of irons, the sociable hum of the electric carts. He listened. . . .
>
> He turned his head. Beyond the glade the pine forest was as dark as twilight except for a single poplar which caught the sun. . . .
>
> Lifting the three-iron slowly and watching it all the while, once again he held it like a shotgun at rest, club head high between his chest and arm, shaft resting across his forearm. Now, carefully, as if he were reenacting an event not quite remembered, as if he had forgotten something which his muscles and arms and hands might remember, he swung the shaft of the iron slowly to and fro like the barrel of a shotgun. He stopped and again stood as still as a hunter. Now turning his head and stooping he looked back at the fence.
>
> But he had not forgotten anything. Today for some reason he remembered everything. Everything he saw became a sign of something else. . . .
>
> Only one event had ever happened to him in his life. Everything else that had happened afterwards was a non-event. . . . Stooping now, he was trying to make his body remember what had happened.
>
> The boy had gone through the fence first . . . (Ibid., 50–2).

And then as Will stands in the dark woods the memory of it all comes back to him as he has been willing to allow it to.

The memory of going as he sometimes did with his father to hunt quail.

Of his father doing a strange thing while out there—hugging him and patting him, saying "Do you trust me?"

Of the pursuit of two birds into a thicket with Will going around the thicket in one direction and his father in the other.

Of hearing the whir of wings and first shot.

Of hearing his father reload the double-barrelled Greener and then suddenly hearing another shot.

Of seeing "the muzzle burst and flame spurting from the gun like a picture of a Civil War soldier shooting and even had time to wonder why he had never seen it before, before he heard the whistling and banging in his ear and found himself down in the leaves without knowing how he got there." (Ibid., 56)

The boy then hears his father's gun being reloaded and then a third shot and silence. As it happened, the shot that hit Will merely grazed his cheek. He got up, went back, and in a few minutes found his father half-laying, half-sitting up against a tree, unconscious with the butt of his shotgun between his legs, sticking out from under his hunting jacket. He is not mortally wounded, and Will finds help to get him home. His father later passes it all off as a hunting accident, and until now Will apparently has successfully "forgotten it" in the same way. Now on the golf course and in the same kind of woods, Will chooses to face it and see it for what it was. It takes time, however, and Will grapples with the memories throughout the course of the narrative.

By the act of choosing despair, choosing to stay with the dread memories, Will begins to recover himself: "Strange to say at the very moment of his remembering the distant past the meaning of his present life becomes clear to him, instantly and without the least surprise as if he had known it all along but had not until now taken the trouble to know that he knew." He has awakened to himself and sees that the twenty years spent in trying to get free of his father by marrying "a rich, hardheaded, plain, decent, crippled pious upstate Utica, New York, woman, practicing Trusts and Estates Law in a paneled office on Wall Street, etc. . . . could just as easily have been a long night's dream . . ." (Ibid., 72–3)

Through his allowing the memories to return and dealing with them he also comes to terms with his father who, he sees, did what he did out of a misguided effort to enable his son not to have to live in the paltry, senseless world that he saw. Will muses, "and now for the first time since that day you cursed me by the fence and grabbed my gun, I don't hate you. We're together after all. Silence. Very well. At last I know why I feel better holding a shotgun than a three iron." A little later on in the narrative he again remembers his father lying in the pinoak swamp. "His father did not speak but in his eyes there were both sorrow and certitude. 'Now you know,' the eyes said. 'I'm sorry. I was trying to tell you something and I didn't. Now you'll have to find out for yourself. I'm sorry.' Very well, he thought, I found out. Now I know what to do" (Ibid., 122–3). We find that, though he is later once again fearfully tempted to suicide, he resists, and it is because now he knows what to do. He has come to terms with his father and with death, and he opts for life. Again we can see that he has begun to recover himself when he asks,

> How did it happen that now for the first time in his life he could see everything so clearly? Something had given him leave to live in the present. Not once in his entire life had he allowed himself to come to rest in the quiet center of himself but had forever cast himself forward from some dark past he did not remember to a future which did not exist. Not once had he been present for his life. So his life had passed like a dream.
>
> Is it possible for people to miss their lives in the same way one misses a plane? And how is it that death, the nearness of death, can restore a missed life? (Ibid., 123–4)

The despair allows a new seeing and a new naming, an action of symbolization, which restores Will's selfhood. Later in the story he comes to a moment in which he is able to name just what it is that constitutes the death in this life that his father had sought to escape and to help his son escape. The reader will recall Will's gleeful new seeing described in an earlier section when he discovers that the name of the enemy is death, "not the death of dying but the living death," including "Death in the guise of love, . . . in the guise of old Christendom in

Carolina, . . . Death in the form of isms and asms" (Ibid., 272–3).

Will's coming to himself is also marked by his

> belated recognition of my life-long dependency on this or that person, like my father or yourself (who I supposed knew more than I did) or on this or that book or theory like Dr. Freud's (which I thought might hold the Great Secret of Life, as if there were such a thing). My equally belated discovery is the total failure, fecklessness, and assholedness of people in general and in particular just those people I had looked to. This includes you. (Ibid., 187)

In his middle years Will looks back on twenty years of non-living in aesthetic immediacy, of money earning, and upper-class diversion which seems to him, in retrospect, like a dream. In all of this he was trying to forget the one event of his life with which he had to come to terms. However, he cannot repress the despairing memory forever, and he finally allows it to come into his consciousness. He grapples with it and it enables him to name the enemy: death in life in its various guises of human paltriness. But the marvel is that in this seeing and naming he overcomes the "death" and acquires his sovereign selfhood.

Percy's stories offer multiple examples of this movement to selfhood made possible by the intensification of "despair." Binx Bolling is seen making it several times, once after the war when he broke with the aesthetic diversions of his bachelor friends with whom he had been hiking on the Appalachian Trail, reading poetry, drinking booze. "For some reason I sank into a deep melancholy," says Binx. And then . . . , "I will say good bye and wish you well. I think I will go back to New Orleans and live in Gentilly" (M, 41–2). Through accepting the despair, instead of stifling it with his pals, he is enabled to perform the act that is the beginning of selfhood.

The young Will Barrett makes the break while a junior at Princeton. The phoniness of the way his friends there live, the enslaving traditions of the place, going back to his father and grandfather when they were students, all work to undermine Will's selfhood. "An immense melancholy overtook him. It was, he knew, the very time of life one is supposed to treasure most, a time of questing and roistering, the prime and pride of youth." And his fellow students?

> They too knew it was the best years of their lives and they were enjoying themselves accordingly ... At last, and despite him-self, he uttered a loud groan, which startled him and momen-tarily silenced his classmates. "Hm," he muttered and peered at his eyeballs in the mirror. "This is no place for me for another half-hour, let alone two years." Forty minutes later he sat on a bus, happy as a lark, bound for New York, where he lived quite contentedly at the Y.M.C.A. (*TLG*, 13, 15).

Again the intensification of despair, and the choosing to allow it to intensify, enables new seeing and naming. Will articulates to himself the phoniness that he sees and from which he final-ly acts to free himself. He has become a sovereign self living quite contentedly at a Y.M.C.A. just off Central Park.

SEEING AND ACTING

One makes the break from living in passive attachment to what is imposed from the outside and begins to act on one's own. The individual moves into a decisively new mode of ex-istence, indeed, one so radically new that Kierkegaard and Per-cy describe it as moving from death into life. What are the characteristics of this new mode of existence? In Kierkegaard's terminology the individual has made the decisive break to selfhood and has "leaped" into the ethical stage, there to act for the first time as a responsible person in the world. But this is not yet the second decisive leap into God-relationship, which is the religious stage.

It is Percy's gift, his keen insight into the way people live, to see and portray in his characters the basic human movements that Kierkegaard identified. In the remainder of this chapter we shall look at the figure in Percy's fiction who most clearly exemplifies the new way of living enabled by the break with immediacy. It is none other than young Will Barrett as he appears in the earlier novel, *The Last Gentleman*. We have already met the younger Will in previous discussions of angelism, and examples were drawn from his occasional lapses back into that state. However, Will in *The Last Gentleman* is portrayed as one who has essentially broken with immediacy and made the first decisive leap into selfhood. The way in which he lives can provide us with the most important characteristics of "living" as opposed to being "dead, dead, dead."

The most striking thing about Will is that "like the sole survivor of a bombed building, he had no secondhand opinions and he could see things afresh." He is described as "the sentient engineer, whose sole gift, after all, was the knack of divining persons and situations" (*TLG*, 11, 47). This is also, certainly, Walker Percy's great gift. The ability to see afresh is what enables Will to live creatively, particularly in his relationships with people.

Ellen Douglas, a commentator on Percy's work brings out the results of Will's ability to see:

> But there is one thing about Barrett that Sutter has not seen; indeed that none of these people has seen. He is that impossible creation of fiction, a good man. Never once in all the course of the book does he act in his own interest—always in the interest of someone else, and always directly, because he cares about or cannot bear to hurt or offend the other person. In him manners are truly morals (*WPG*, 19).

In a published interview with Percy, the novelist Ashley Brown likened Barrett to Dostoevsky's "idiot" and asked if a Prince Myshkin is not difficult to make convincing, noting that "Will Barrett is certainly one of the few 'good' characters to turn up in recent fiction." Percy acknowledged that Will "bears a conscious kinship to Prince Myshkin," saying that he "wanted to portray a young man who could see things afresh" (*Shen*, 6).

How then does Will Barrett live? We shall first look at several aspects of this, examining in more detail how this way of living is manifested in a relationship with a particular friend. The author's descriptions of Will in the narrative are sprinkled with such phrases as "unusual young man," "sentient engineer," and "very prescient person." Val, the Vaught sister, who is a nun of sorts, says to him: "Barrett, look. I know that you are a highly intelligent and intuitive man, and that you have a gift for fathoming people. Isn't that true?" And on one occasion Rita, Sutter's ex, says to him: "You know, sometimes I have the feeling, Lance Corporal, that you are on-to all of us, onto our most private selves." Finally, it is said of him by the narrator that he "knew two things not many people know. He knew how to listen and he knew how to get at that most secret and aggrieved enterprise upon which almost everybody is embarked." (TLG, 3, 152, 287)

Thus, Will is a very unusual person indeed; he is what everyone needs from others and wants to be himself: he has a unique ability to be in touch with and related to life and other persons. Gabriel Marcel, whose influence Percy acknowledges, compares this perfection of human existence to the sensory receptivity of a living organism to its surroundings:

> I confine myself in this context to stressing the following preliminary condition: I must somehow make room for the other in myself; if I am completely absorbed in myself, concentrated on my sensations, feelings, anxieties, it will obviously be impossible for me to receive, to incorporate in myself, the message of the other. What I called incohesion a moment ago here assumes the form of disposability; thus we are indirectly brought to the question whether there is not a basis for granting the existence of a fundamental analogy between the sensory receptivity of a living being exposed to the solicitation of his surroundings and the disposability of a consciousness capable of caring for another person (CF, 87).

Marcel makes clear, however, that the human act of being open to another is not simply the passive receiving of a mental and emotional imprint, as in the case of a sub-human organism; it involves the free choice of opening to the other and thereby giving of oneself. The soliciting presence of another person can be refused but when it is, "it is as though I walled myself up." A person, then, is aroused to action by the call of things that come upon him: persons, events, demands for responsible decision. As Marcel puts it, "You invite me to create myself. You are this very invitation." This invitation to a self-creating act is essentially what happened when Binx saw the dung-beetle, when the commuter sees his hand after suffering the heart attack, and when Will sees Kitty through the telescope and falls in love with her. Will sees and responds to person-and-event summonses in sharp contrast to Sutter, who tends to shut himself off from his surroundings in pursuit of his own abstractions. Will at Princeton sees what is happening—his phony friends, the dead weight of the tradition of the place—and in his despair at this he is enabled to act.

By being open and choosing to act, Will is by that very fact different from others, sometimes painfully so. On one occasion he reflects, "But if there is nothing wrong with me . . . then there is something wrong with the world. And if there is nothing wrong with the world, then I have wasted my life and that is the worst mistake of all" (*TLG*, 76). Kierkegaard's central vision is the need to will to be different if one is to become one's own self. In his Journal, in which we can be sure we read Kierkegaard straight instead of through the sometimes ambiguous voices of his characters, he says:

> O my God. . . . It is not difference I must pray myself out of, that is not the task, but alas, I shall never know security, which consists in being like others. No, I remain different. There I remain with Thee—and verily I know its happiness; the only thing that has made me anxious was the thought that possibly the task was another, namely that I should escape from that unlikeness, a thought which may very well have been prompted by the wish to make my life secure (*JD*, 1252).

Will, like all of Percy's protagonists, has what would normally be regarded as disabilities. In the interview with Ashley Brown, Percy says of him, "in the conventional view of things he is very sick. . . . The reader is free to see him as a sick man among healthy business men or as a sane pilgrim in a mad world" (*Shen*, 7). Percy, of course, is saying that what we regard as normal is really "dead, dead, dead," while the one who really sees what is going on and begins to search may develop symptoms because he has cast loose the support of the crowd. More will be said about this in the final chapter when we consider the religious mode of existence.

The very insecurity of seeing and acting on one's own makes

one aware of his or her need, and this in turn makes the individual open to others. We see this in all of Percy's protagonists. Binx insists that he always cultivates contacts with others—the ticket-taker at the movie theatre, for example—"for good selfish reasons" (M, 75). Dr. Thomas More sees his "shakiness" as the source of his sensitivity to the problems of his patients:

> It is my misfortune—and blessing—that I suffer from both liberal and conservative complaints, e.g., both morning terror and large bowel disorders, excessive abstraction and unreasonable rages, alternating impotence and satyriasis. So that at one and the same time I have great sympathy for my patients and lead a fairly miserable life (LIR, 20).

Young Will Barrett's revealing his tendency toward amnesia to Kitty was what made her realize that he was not after "some boy-girl thing" and made her see him in a new way. And certainly it is his own problem with himself that enables the later middle-aged Will to be disposable to the twenty-year-old Allie, recently escaped from a mental hospital.

Percy's sketches of the younger Will are filled with humor, and yet they present this essentially "good" young man as one who is completely at the disposal of others. A hilarious sequence occurs during Will's hitchhiking trip from New York City to Alabama to rejoin the Vaught family, who have left him behind. He was picked up on the New Jersey Turnpike by what appears to be a middle-aged Negro in a "bottle-green Chevrolet, an old '58 Junebug [which] passed and hesitated, the driver's foot lifting and the carburator sucking wind, speeded up and hesitated again." The driver was "a light-colored high-stomached Negro dressed in a good brown suit, no doubt a preacher or a teacher." After a brief conversation, however, the sentient engineer noticed that "something was amiss here." It develops that the driver is a "pseudo-Negro." He is Forney Aiken, a well-known white news photographer heading south to do a story on blacks living there. It may be that Percy intends Forney's name to be a play on words as a symbol of so much of what repels the author in modern America. Forney lives in the aesthetic mode and is typically obsessed with sex.

He tells Will with relish, for example, about a novelist friend's latest book which, he says, "is about _____ing."

It is Forney's daughter, Muzh, to whom Will eventually responds in a creative way through his gift of seeing. They first meet in Forney's pool, where she is soon brushing against him with her knees. He "seized her through her thick parts, fell upon her as much from weakness as desire, fainted upon her, the fine brown berry of a girl she was. 'Zut alors,' she cried softly." Later when Forney said he would lend him the book *Love*, "The engineer groaned, What the devil does he mean telling me it's about _____ing? Is _____ing a joking matter? Am I to understand I am free to _____ his daughter? Or do we speak of _____ing man to man, jokingly, literally, with no thought of _____ing anyone in the vicinity? His radar boggled." That night just after he had gone to bed a knock came at the door; it was Muzh in a shorty nightgown delivering *Love*!

> "Thank you," said the engineer, laughing heartily; and when she had left went reeling about the room like Rooney Lee after the battle of Seven Days. What saved him in the end was not only Southern Chivalry but Yankee good sense. Muzh he *saw* all at once and belatedly, as she might have been seen by **her** classmates, as a horsy, good-natured, sisterly sort. She was, as they say in the North, a good kid. And so it was permitted him to leave her alone and to excuse himself. What a relief. He wiped his brow (*TLG*, 137, emphasis added).

What saved him from doing what would not have been good for her, nor for himself, was Will's seeing her for what she was—a "sisterly sort"—and therefore that she was not asking for his body as he had first thought. Sometime earlier he had taken the opposite course with Kitty, who had offered herself to him in Central Park, and he did it out of concern for her feelings: "He kissed her with an amiable passion, mainly concerned now to bear with her, serve her anticness as gracefully as he could. He aimed to guard her against her own embarrassment."

We may be helped to appreciate Will's unique caring for others by means of a contrast. Rita Vaught and he react quite differently to David, the seventeen-year-old black butler in the Vaught's household. David had not yet "caught onto either the

Negro way or the white way." He was always answering advertisements in magazines like *"Learn Electronics! Alert Young Men Needed!"* Will sees David's naiveté and vulnerability. He says, "You think they're going to treat you well, you act like you're baby brother at home. Christ, they're not going to treat you well." One day David decided he wanted to be a sportscaster. "The engineer groaned aloud. Sportscaster for Christ's sake; six feet six, black as pitch, speech like molasses in the mouth, and he wanted to be a sportscaster." Will sees David, sees how he can be hurt, and tries to help him. How different is Rita's response, which does not really see David but sees primarily herself in a helping role:

> Now he couldn't help overhearing Rita, who was telling David earnestly about so-and-so she knew at CBS, a sweet, wonderful guy who might be able to help him, at least suggest a good sportscasting school (Ibid., 217).

A last humorous example of Will's sensitivity is an exchange between him and Lamar Thigpen, an acquaintance of the Vaught family in Alabama.

> They were headed back to the hearts game but Lamar Thigpen caught them. "Did you ever hear about this alligator who went into a restaurant?" He took them by the neck and drew them close as lovers.
> "No, I didn't," said the courteous engineer, though he had. Jokes always made him nervous. He had to attend to the perilous needs of the joke-teller. Jamie dispensed himself and paid no attention: I'm sick and I don't have to oblige anybody.
> "The waitress came over and brought him a menu. So this alligator says to her: do yall serve niggers in here? She says yes, we do. So he says, O.K. I'll take two." . . .
> "That's all right, Mr. Thigpen," said the engineer while the other held him close as a lover and gazed hungrily at his cheek. (Ibid., 221–2)

Unlike Jamie, who "paid no attention," Will's awareness of Lamar's "terrible needs," make it necessary for him to affirm the joke-teller in spite of his aversion to the joke. Lamar's need of acceptance is the special grace that enables Will's caring.

THE TWO

It is one-on-one fellowship, relationship, ultimately friendship, that Percy sees as the fundamental enabler of life at the human level. Each of his fictional protagonists moves toward such relationship. One of the two epigraphs to *The Last Gentleman*, the other being from Kierkegaard, points up this theme. It is from Romano Guardini's *The End of the Modern World:*

> ... We know now that the modern world is coming to an end ... at the same time, the unbeliever will emerge from the fogs of secularism. He will cease to reap benefit from the values and forces developed by the very Revelation he denies ... Loneliness in faith will be terrible. Love will disappear from the face of the public world, but the more precious will be that love which flows from one lonely person to another ... the world to come will be filled with animosity and danger, but it will be a world open and clean.

This inter-subjectivity of two persons is, in Percy's view, founded in their mutual acts of symbolization. Percy notes two things about symbolization, beyond the already mentioned centrality of its role as the act that creates the sovereign self: first, that a person cannot perform this action alone, and, second, that "holding a symbol in common with another person establishes a relationship not only between man and object but also between man and man" (*Ren,* 209). As Percy states emphatically:

> *Symbolization is of its very essence an intersubjectivity.* If there were only one person in the world, symbolization could not conceivably occur (but signification could); for my discovery of water as something derives from your telling me so, that this is water for you too. The act of symbolization is an affirmation: yes, this is water! My excitement derives from the discovery that it is there for you and me and that it is the same thing for you and me. Every act of symbolization thereafter, whether it be language, art, science, or even thought, must occur either in the presence of a real you or an ideal you for whom the symbol is intended as meaningful (*MB,* 281).

Percy asserts that the relationship between the two persons is the direct result of their sharing in this act: "But surely it is that the 'We are' follows upon and is mediated by the symbolization, the joint affirmation that this is water." When two people share a symbol together in this way they are, says Percy, "co-celebrants of being" as, for example, in the following:

> When a tribesman utters a single word which means the-sun-shining-through-a-hole-in-the-clouds-in-a-certain-way, he is combining the offices of poet and scientist. His fellow tribesmen know what he means. We have no word for it because we have long since analyzed the situation into its component elements. But we need to have a word for it, and it is the office of a poet to give us a word. If he is a good poet and names something which we secretly and privately know but have not named, we rejoice at the naming and say, Yes! I know what you mean. Once again we are co-celebrants of being (*Pers*, 156).

This co-celebration happens continuously between persons and is essential to the fabric of human life. Dr. Thomas More, the protagonist of *Love in the Ruins*, is temporarily a patient in the mental ward of the local hospital. He articulates his own feeling by means of an unusual symbol. A fellow patient shares it with him and the two who had been lonely "I's" become a "We" in that moment:

> Sitting here in the day room the day after Christmas next to a mangy pine tree decorated with varicolored Kleenex (no glass!), the stereo-V showing the Blue-Gray game and rolling flip flip flip, my hands on my knees and wrists bandaged, I felt so bad that I groaned aloud an Old Testament lamentation AAAA-EOOOOOW! to which responded a great silent black man sitting next to me on the blocky couch: "Ain't it the truth though" (*LIR*, 105).

The one thing that cannot be captured in a symbol is a person, says Percy, either one's self or another: "I, who symbolize the world in order to know it, am destined to remain forever unknown to myself" (*MB*, 283). The danger of striving for the security of symbolizing oneself is the tendency to limit oneself to a particular self-image, and thereby in fact limit the self; or, one impersonates the kind of self he or she thinks is acceptable, thereby losing the self. If I try in this way to capture another person as an object, there can be no real relationship.

On the other hand, when we share the naming or understanding of something else we become companions. The other person has a "unique and indispensable role in the sustaining and validation of my consciousness."

> The Thou is at once the source of my consciousness, the companion and co-celebrant of my discovery of being—and the sole threat to my unauthentic constitution of myself. (Ibid., 285)

This is a compelling statement of the utter necessity of other persons to the proper living of one's life, including the others' role in revealing one's own self-deceptions. Percy rivals Sartre in his description here of how the mere look or stare of another person unmasks the pretender:

> My vulnerability before the look derives from the aboriginal triadic communion of consciousness. The Thou is the knower, the namer, the co-inspector with me of the common thing and the authority for its name. Whatever devious constitution of self I have been able to arrive at, whatever my "self-system," my impersonation, it melts away before the steady gaze of another. (Ibid.)

Again, let us turn to concrete human beings to see how some of this looks in real life. The younger Will Barrett and Jamie in *The Last Gentleman* can show us. As this story opened, Will, a 25-year-old Alabaman, was living in New York City at the Central Park Y.M.C.A. and working at night as a maintenance engineeer, "a kind of janitor," at Macy's. A high-powered telescope, which Will has bought with his last remaining savings, plays an important role in the opening pages, and symbolizes the author's view that real seeing cannot be taken for granted. It must be enabled by something other than one's self.

> . . . he couldn't help attributing magical properties to the telescope. It had to do with its being German, with fabled German craftsmen, gnomic slow-handed old men in the Harz Mountains. These lenses did not transmit light merely. They penetrated to the heart of things.
>
> The conviction grew upon him that his very life would be changed if he owned the telescope. (*TLG*, 28)

As he focused the telescope on a building across the park he saw the bricks as if seeing bricks for the first time:

> They gained in value. Every grain and crack and excresence became available. Beyond any doubt, he said to himself, this proves that bricks, as well as other things, are not as accessible as they used to be. Special measures were needed to recover them.
>
> The telescope recovered them. (Ibid., 30)

Shortly thereafter Will sees Kitty Vaught in Central Park through his telescope and, as we have noted previously, falls in love with her at first sight. Not many days pass before Will, in the process of following Kitty whom he had not yet even talked to, finds himself in a Washington Heights hospital room. Kitty's younger brother Jamie, a high school senior, is the patient. Mr. and Mrs. Vaught have brought him up from their home in Alabama for treatment for a severe form of mononucleosis which has steadily worsened during the past year. It is a humorous and happy scene as Will reverts to his Alabama ways in falling into quick acquaintance with the family.

A few days later Will hits upon the idea of lending Jamie the telescope for his birthday. He brings it and sets it up for Jamie at the window. The stage is set for a focused portrayal of relationship taking place as the result of shared symbolization.

> The patient had only to prop himself on an elbow and look down into the prism. A little disc of light played about his pupil. The engineer watched him watch: now he, Jamie, would be seeing it, the brilliant theater bigger and better than life. Picnickers they were, a family deployed on a shelf of granite above the Hudson. The father held a can of beer.
>
> Once Jamie looked up for a second, searched his face for a sign: did he really see what he saw? The engineer nodded. Yes, he saw.
>
> "What kind of beer is he drinking?" he asked Jamie.
>
> "Rheingold," said Jamie. (Ibid., 73)

Jamie looks up for affirmation and sharing in the view he sees: they mutually *name* what he sees—the father in the family below is drinking—Rheingold! They are co-celebrating being. "My excitement," says Percy, "derives from the discovery that it is there for you and me and that it is the same thing for you and me" (*MB*, 281). The effect on Jamie is noticeable. His mother "couldn't get over it. . . . 'Would you look at the color in that child's face!' " (*TLG*, 74). His father has seen it, too, and takes Will outside to ask him to join them and be Jamie's tutor and companion. "I just saw what effect you had on him," he says. "That's the first time I've seen that boy perk up since I been up here." This is a clear characterization of Percy's view that relationship, through shared symbolization, is what gives life.

The friendship between Will and Jamie develops as they head back to Alabama, just the two of them, in the Vaught Trav-L-Aire camper.

> Nights were best. Then as the thick singing darkness settled about the little caboose which shed its cheerful square of light on the dark soil of old Carolina, they might debark and, with the pleasantest sense of stepping down from the zone of the possible to the zone of the realized, stroll to a service station or fishing camp or grocery store, where they'd have a beer or fill the tank with spring water or lay in eggs and country butter and grits and slab bacon; then back to the camper (Ibid., 154).

Again the telescope tells the reader how they symbolize together:

> He unlimbered the telescope and watched a fifty-foot Chris-Craft beat up the windy Intercoastal. A man sat in the stern reading the *Wall Street Journal*. "Dow Jones, 894—" read the engineer. What about cotton futures, he wondered.
> He called Jamie over. "Look how he pops his jaw and crosses his legs with the crease of his britches pulled out of the way."
> "Yes," said Jamie, registering and savoring what the engineer registered and savored. *Yes, you and I know something the man in the Chris-Craft will never know.* "What are we going to do when we get home?" (Ibid., 155)

What they *know* is each other, whereas the man in the Chris-Craft sits alone.

This was the game they played: the sentient tutor knowing quite well how to strike the dread unsounded chords of adolescence, the youth registering, his mouth parted slightly, fingernails brushing backward across his face. *Yes, and that was the wonder of it, that what was private and unspeakable before is speakable now because you speak it.* (Ibid.)

Clearly Percy is portraying human relatedness growing out of the shared act of symbolizing or naming reality. A great joy has come into Jamie, whose parents hadn't seen him so perked up in weeks. " 'Yes, me too,' nodded the youth, eyes focused happily on the bright note of agreement in the air between them."

A particularly touching and humorous example of the same appears near the end of the story when Will has just gotten back together with Jamie—this time in a hospital in Santa Fe. Jamie is worse. They are talking about Sutter, Jamie's older brother, who had brought him out to Santa Fe to die:

> Jamie began to speak fondly of Sutter, catching his breath now and then in his new warrior style. "You ought to see that rascal," said Jamie, shaking his head.
>
> The engineer listened smilingly as Jamie told of Sutter's guest ranch whose cottages had such names as O.K. Corral and Boot Hill. Sutter lived at Doc's. "Though it's called a guest ranch, it's really a way station for grass widows. Ol' Sutter is busy as a one-armed paperhanger."
>
> "I imagine," said the engineer fondly and gloomily . . .
>
> "Have you see him?" asks Jamie.
>
> "Yes." The engineer told of coming upon Sutter just after he bought two fifths of Two Natural. *"Does he still drink bad whiskey?"*
>
> *"Oh Christ,"* whispered Jamie *joyfully and began to thrash his legs as of old* (Ibid., 348, 49—emphasis added).

Once again, a shared image and the joy and relationship it brings.

In sharp contrast to the relatedness that gives life and joy to Jamie and Will is the lack of the same between Jamie and other members of his family. Walker Percy, in the interview cited, says, "They're all after Jamie. But it's Barrett who is the instrument of the boy's salvation" (*Shen*, 8). Percy is referring particularly to Sutter, Rita, and Val. Sutter, as we have seen, is unable to be close to anyone so absorbed is he in himself and his own ideas. He does not really see Jamie or see the world through Jamie's eyes but attempts to impose his own idea of what is best for him. His desire that Jamie "die well" was clearly a projection of his own urge to be the sole disposer of his own life. He did not ask Jamie what he wanted and refused to listen to other family members. Sutter was in bondage to an *idée fixe.*

Both Val and Rita fail to be in touch with Jamie for the same reason that Sutter failed. They all exist in the aesthetic immediacy of abstraction—angelism. It is repeatedly made clear that for Rita the real is the abstraction, the generality, not the particular concrete person or event. Jamie is demoted to a mere specimen of the general and therefore not an object of value in her eyes. In the following she is speaking of Jamie's impending death.

> "So it's not such a big thing," she said softly.
> "One small adolescent as against the thirty thousand Japanese children we polished off."
> "How's that?" said the engineer cupping his good ear.
> "At Hiroshima and Nagasaki."
> "I don't, ah—" (*TLG*, 90).

Later her ex-husband, Sutter, asks Rita, "What do you really care what happens to Jamie?"

> "I care."
> "Tell me honestly what difference it makes to you whether Jimmy lives or dies."
> The engineer was shocked, but Rita replied routinely. "You know very well there is no use in my answering you. Except to say that there is such a thing as concern and there is such a thing as preference for life over death. I do not desire death; mine, yours, or Jamie's." (Ibid., 234)

It is not difficult to see why she had no real relationship with Jamie. Her extreme lack of awareness of or kinship with others is brought out by the fact that her only thought with respect to Jamie is to use the circumstances of his departure with Sutter to induce Will to follow them so that she can have Kitty to herself. She is unable to see Jamie as another person—an end in himself.

Val, the Vaught sister and nun, also exists in intellectual immediacy. She is hooked on religious ideas and is therefore neither in touch with persons nor, presumably, with God. Will has just told Val that he is on his way West to find Jamie:

> It came to him for the second time that he didn't like her, particularly her absorption with the hawk. It was a chicken hawk with an old rusty shoulder and a black nostril. She attended to the hawk with a buzzing antic manner which irritated him. It scandalized him slightly, like the Pope making a fuss over a canary. He was afraid she might call the hawk by some such name as Saint Blaise. (Ibid., 285)

Val is interested in only one thing in connection with Jamie: that he be baptized. She is intent to have this imposed upon him whether or not he should agree. Finally she "lapsed into her old smiling thrumming Papal inwardness, wherein she dispensed herself so that she might take note of God's creatures, small objects and such. She went back to the hawk and he left." So by her constant absorption in religious antics—"an enthusiast of a certain sort . . . like a collector of 1928 Model T radiator caps"—Val cuts herself off from humanity. It is no wonder that Jamie had refused to listen to her when she tried to tell him about "the economy of salvation."

In sharp contrast—Will is speaking to Jamie:

> "Rita spoke to me today. Do you know what she wants us to do?"
> "Yes."
> "Is that what you want to do?"
> Again he heard the slight break in breathing, the little risible and incredulous sound he seemed to call forth from people. (Ibid., 115)

Will calls forth an incredulous reaction from people precisely because he characteristically treats them as persons, lets them be who they are and responds to them. He never deceives Jamie in order to make him feel good. When they arm-wrestled, "The engineer, who never faked with Jamie, put him down quickly. But Jamie was surprisingly strong." (Ibid., 116)

It is in the final scene between the two friends that Percy seems to indicate that a breakthrough to a God-relationship took place in Jamie, again with his essential co-celebrant of being in the person of Will. True to his promise to Val, Will has found the hospital chaplain, a Roman Catholic priest, and brought him to baptize Jamie before he dies. Sutter too is present and reluctantly tells the priest to go ahead with the baptism. Will stands close to Jamie and has to repeat for the priest Jamie's almost inaudible responses. The priest says,

> "I have been asked by your sister to administer to you the sacrament of baptism. Do you wish to receive it?"
> The engineer frowned. Wasn't the priest putting it a bit formally? . . .
> "Excuse me, Father," said the sentient engineer. "He said 'what.' "
> "Oh," said the priest and turned both fists out and opened the palms. "Do you accept the truth that God exists and that He made you and loves you and that He made the world so that you might enjoy its beauty and that He himself is your final end and happiness, that He loved you so much that He sent His only Son to die for you . . ."
> "Is that true?" said Jamie clearly, opening his eyes and goggling. To the engineer's dismay the youth turned to him (Ibid., 387–8).

Jamie then nods his "yes" to Will and after receiving the sacramental action holds onto the priest's hand and says, "Don't let me go." It may be presumed he has made the leap into the religious mode—the leap of faith. In the crucial seeing and naming that he did in responding to the priest, Will was the other one who saw and named with him as they had done so many times before. As Percy commented, Barrett was the instrument of Jamie's salvation—such are the lengths to which real human relatedness can go.

Although Will has made the first movement to selfhood through his break with immediacy, he has not yet made the second into "selfhood before God," that is, the religious stage of existence. That he eventually moves into this "second immediacy," as Kierkegaard sometimes calls the religious stage, is the burden of this novel as it is of Percy's other stories. The second breakthrough always comes at the culmination of the protagonist's passionate quest. It is to this that we now turn our attention.

Chapter 8

Religious Existence— *Kierkegaard*

What does Kierkegaard have to tell us of what it is to live in the religious modality? His entire work is concerned with illuminating the way to and the characteristics of this highest possibility of human existence. Personal choice and action are again central, but the movement to faith, he insists, is only possible through an action beyond the human, that is through the gift of God himself.

It is as true of the religious as it is of the ethical stage that what is important for the person is not what he knows but the way in which he lives his life. Kierkegaard remarks that the person who prays to an idol in all sincerity and with resolve to act upon what he believes is nearer the truth than the person who in a superficial way attends Christian worship. Kierkegaard's sometimes misunderstood assertion that "subjectivity is truth" expresses this. It does not mean that truth is purely subjective and can be whatever anyone wants it to be. By "subjectivity is truth" he means that when a person strives to live in response to what his deepest inner being tells him, this striving is truth. Kierkegaard expresses it another way when he says "inwardness is truth." Continual response to the presence of the eternal, rejecting other enticements, is essentially what constitutes religious existence. Kierkegaard entitled one of his religious works: *Purity of Heart Is To Will One Thing*. Thus religious existence is a *way* of living, not a matter of believing the right things.

How then does one find himself in this deepest and freest of all levels of human existence? As despair was the "movement in the clock" out of the aesthetic into the ethical stage, so it is also in the leap from the ethical to the religious. Despair is the condition that all is not well within oneself and in one's life. Why does the ethical stage come to this end? Because, says Kierkegaard, no one is able to meet the infinite demands of the ethical. The young aesthete who, by "choosing despair," has recovered himself and begins a responsible life, is at first confident that he can achieve a moral life. Kierkegaard indentifies "struggle and victory" as the central characteristic of the ethical stage. To his chagrin however, if he is honest with himself, the ethicist realizes that he fails repeatedly in this struggle. "The requirement is so infinite, " says Kierkegaard, "that the individual always goes bankrupt." (*SLW*, 430). In his failure, his despair intensifies and it is then that he may be enabled to "leap" to the religious.

What is this leap itself like? Kierkegaard says that as the person allows his sense of despair to deepen, he or she becomes aware of a new dimension to which he is related and which calls forth desire and love. He may call it the Good, he may call it Truth, or he may call it God. In the ethical mode it was the universal ethical demand, the expectations of the culture laid upon him from the outside which he strove to achieve. Now it is an inner summons spoken to him alone. In response to this he may be required to suspend, at times, the standards of conventional morality.

A comparison between two of Kierkegaard's fictional characters may help clarify the distinction between the ethicist's striving to meet external ethical demands and the religious response to inwardness. Judge William of *Either/Or* lives in the former mode. He believes in God, but he conceives of him impersonally, simply as the Power which stands behind the universal ethical imperative. Kierkegaard's Abraham, on the other hand, is in the religious mode. He becomes aware of God personally calling him to put all else aside in order to answer a personal demand upon himself. God tells him to take his son

Isaac, go to the top of Mount Moriah and there to slay his son as a sacrificial offering. Abraham sets out in silent obedience. Finally, when all has been prepared he raises the knife. At the last moment, however, God stays his hand. The point is clear: one must be willing to put all else aside in response to God's inner call. He must, as Kierkegaard puts it, have "an absolute relation to the Absolute and a relative relation to the relative." If such a relationship is only a figment of one's imagination, as the unbeliever would say, then, of course, says Kierkegaard, "Abraham is lost; he can only be understood as intending to murder his son" (FT, 66).

Abraham is an extreme and culturally conditioned example, but he is central to Kierkegaard's understanding of the religious. He has become aware of himself as personally confronted by God's requirement and can do no other. It is then that the universal ethical expectation may itself become the temptation. Kierkegaard experienced this in his break with Regine. His temptation was to do what everyone else would have felt was the only right thing to do and marry her. He reflects that this sort of thing "remains to all eternity a paradox, inaccessible to thought."

> Faith is precisely this paradox, that the individual as the particular is higher than the universal, is justified over against it, is not subordinate but superior . . . for the fact that the individual as the particular stands in an absolute relation to the absolute. (Ibid.)

The poet W.H. Auden says it another way: "The I signifies nothing if it does not become the 'thou' to whom eternity speaks and says: 'Thou shalt, thou shalt, thou shalt.'"

Life in the religious mode itself moves through several stages. Kierkegaard describes what he calls the "infinite double movement" which consists of the "movement of infinite resignation" and the "movement of faith." The first of the two movements is the necessary precondition for the second. Beyond these two the final movement of the religious stage, says Kierkegaard, is that which takes one into specifically Christian faith.

THE MOVEMENT OF INFINITE RESIGNATION

In his intention to sacrifice Isaac, Abraham is acting in "infinite resignation." In doing so he is renouncing his "claim to the love which is the content of his life" (*FT*, 57). Isaac was the only child of Abraham and Sarah's old age. Only Abraham, not Sarah, received God's fearful command to sacrifice him, and he does it "for God's sake, and for his own sake."

> He did it for God's sake because God required this proof of his faith; for his own sake he did it in order that he might furnish the proof. (Ibid., 70)

The temptation to draw back would certainly be enforced by the universally recognized requirement that one must not harm, certainly not murder, his own son. Kierkegaard contrasts Abraham with the tragic heroes of literature who act in ways that are generally recognized as exemplary. They live in the ethical mode in which "the ethical is the divine" and is understood as valid by all. Abraham however, must do otherwise.

> The ethical expression for what Abraham did is, that he would murder Isaac; the religious expression is, that he would sacrifice Isaac; but precisely in this contradiction consists the dread which can well make a man sleepless, and yet Abraham is not what he is without this dread. (Ibid., 41)

Abraham suffers the fear and trembling, the dread that he might have "misunderstood the deity . . . what (then) can save him?" All of this and more constitutes his infinite resignation. Kierkegaard is clearly speaking out of his own experience of having felt required to give up Regine, the love of his life.

It is important to note that neither for Kierkegaard nor for Percy does the inner call *necessarily* involve a conscious awareness of "God." To will one thing in the true sense, says Kierkegaard, *is* the God-relationship. He acknowledges that this willing begins at very basic levels. Human love, for example, can "help a man along the right path."

> Faithfully he only willed one thing, his love. For it, he would
> live and die. For it, he would sacrifice all and in it alone he
> would have his eternal reward. Yet the act of being in love is
> still not in the deepest sense the Good. But it may possibly
> become for him a helpful educator, who will finally lead him by
> the possession of his beloved one or perhaps by her loss, in truth
> to will one thing and to will the Good. In this fashion a man is
> educated by many means; and true love is also an education
> toward the Good (*PH*, 40).

To will the Good is to respond to the inner voice and to be ac-
countable to that which one experiences as the eternal. "What
is truth," asks Kierkegaard, "but to live for an idea?" (*JD*, 22).
Again there is no *necessary* God-reference here because,
generally speaking, Kierkegaard uses the concept "idea" to
refer simply to a good cause (*JH* I, 589n). One then can live in
the religious mode without a conscious God-reference. In the
main, the Percean characters who move into the religious
mode seem to do so without an awareness of God being central
to their consciousness. Thus Percy provides hope for modern
man for whom conventional God-awareness seems an increasingly diminished possibility.

In making the movement of infinite resignation, then, one
detaches himself from one love in order to achieve "something
higher" (*FT*, 71). "He brings to naught his joy in the world, he
renounces everything." How and why does he do this? He does
this because he believes in the call that he has received. In the
case of Abraham, says Kierkegaard's pseudonym, Johannes *de
silentio*, "Abraham underneath believed that God would not
require Isaac . . . yet was willing . . . to sacrifice him if it was
required." (Ibid., 46)

This brings us to consideration of what Kierkegaard asserts
is the primary characteristic of religious existence: suffering.

> While aesthetic existence is essentially enjoyment, and ethical
> existence, essentially struggle and victory, religious existence is
> essentially suffering, and that not as a transitional moment, but
> as persisting (*CUP*, 256).

Suffering here is to be understood in the dual sense: first, suffering as the act of allowing something to happen to oneself

("suffer the little children to come unto me") and second, suffering as pain or loss. In religious existence one allows something beyond himself to be the center of his life. In doing so he suffers the loss of certain things in order to gain the highest thing. Kierkegaard insists that without suffering there is no religious existence, in fact, ". . . the more the suffering the more the religious existence." The character Quidam of *Stages Along Life's Way*, is among the religious; his story *Guilty?— Not Guilty?* is said by Kierkegaard to be a "story of suffering." In *Concluding Unscientific Postscript*, which gives his final position on a number of themes, Kierkegaard unequivocally states that suffering is of the essence of religious existence.

> The religious individual has suffering constantly with him. He requires suffering in the same sense that the immediate individual requires fortune, and he requires and has suffering even in the absence of external misfortune. (Ibid., 389)

We should note here, however, what will be amplified later, that is Kierkegaard's insistence that the suffering of the religious is always a suffering underlain by joy.

There is a second source of suffering in religious existence beyond that of giving up the normal supports and pleasures of life. This comes from the awareness of one's continuing failure to live in response to the inner call. He thus feels cut off from the Good for which he had sacrificed everything. He is also cut off from the normal supports that he had given up; they no longer satisfy. He is thus doubly adrift and aware of his guilt for his failure. His desire to hold fast absolutely to the absolute *telos* is just what he cannot fulfil "and precisely this annihilates him . . . his impotence begins" (Ibid, 433). His sense of guilt increases and he dwells upon it inwardly. Kierkegaard thus sees a sense of guilt as central to religious existence. "Precisely thereby is man in a God-relationship," he says (*SLW*, 418). The guilt feelings of the religious mode have a number of sources including even that of successfully doing God's will; the sense of guilt in that case comes because the doer, in his lack of understanding, condemns his own good act. Kierkegaard provides a darkly humorous example of this in the

Stages: "The Quidam of the experiment wished precisely to save life; inspired by pure sympathy he ventures the utmost, and, behold, he gets a murder upon his conscience." (Ibid., 408) The feeling of guilt that accompanies the religious, however, does its own work of deepening the person's self-awareness.

A third cause of suffering in religious existence is that the source of one's new life in this mode is impossible to grasp directly. As Kierkegaard says, "It is a species of suffering, a martyrdom even in peaceful times, to have the happiness of the soul tied to that which the understanding despairs about" (*CUP*, 259) This is even more difficult in our day when God seems more inaccessible than ever.

Finally, a person in religious existence suffers because he cannot effectively communicate to others the meaning of his life. Again consider Abraham and what he felt called upon to do:

> Abraham keeps silent—but he *cannot* speak. Therein lies the distress and anguish . . . The relief of speech is that it translates me into the universal. Now Abraham is able to say the most beautiful things any language can express about how he loves Isaac. But it is not this he has at heart to say, it is the profounder thought that he would sacrifice him because it is a trial. This latter thought no one can understand (*FT*, 122).

Only the individual hears his own "thou shalt," and this he cannot explain. And yet, says Kierkegaard, when one remains in concealment in this way he fails in that other basic human requirement that he live in relationship with others. Abraham bears "the terrible responsibility of solitude," and in his ever present question of "guilty? not guilty?" he suffers (*SLW*, 418). "The martyrdom" of the religious, says Kierkegaard, consists in "living in the world with this inwardness in his breast without having any expression for it" (*CUP*, 453).

This, then, is the movement of infinite resignation.

> The infinite resignation is the last stage prior to faith, so that one who has not made this movement has not faith; for only in the infinite resignation do I become clear to myself with respect to my eternal validity, and only then can there be any question of grasping existence by virtue of faith. (*FT*, 57).

The movement of faith is made possible when the suffering of resignation reaches sufficient intensity. Then "there occurs the prodigy, he makes still another movement more wonderful than all." Despair is once again the catalyst for a leap into fullest human existence.

> My melancholy searches in every direction for the dreadful. Then it grips me with its terror. I cannot and will not flee from it, I must endure the thought; then I find a religious composure, and only then am I free and happy as spirit . . . But he who wills in a religious sense must have a receptive attitude to the terrible, he must open himself to it, and he has only to take care that it does not stop halfway, but that it leads him into the security of the infinite (SLW, 342–3).

Faith is not, as some claim, an "immediate instinct of the heart." It is "something far higher, . . . because it has resignation as its presupposition"(FT, 58). It comes only to those who are willing to struggle for it.

> Here it holds good that only he who works gets the bread, only he who was in anguish finds respose, only he who descends into the underworld rescues the beloved, only he who draws the knife gets Isaac. (Ibid., 38)

The required resignation is something each person can do, enabled by the gift of despair. Let us turn now to consider "the prodigy" itself, the gift of faith, a movement, which again the individual can perform but only by grace.

THE MOVEMENT OF FAITH

Whereas the movement of infinite resignation is essentially a quest, a striving, a putting aside of what hinders, the movement of faith is its result: a new birth. In resignation one gives up everything; in faith one "gets everything back double."

> In resignation I make renunciation of everything, this movement I make by myself, and if I do not make it, it is because I am cowardly and effeminate and without enthusiasm (FT, 59).

In having given up everything the "knight" finds himself at the end cut off and alone. "I ask everyone whether I have had any profit by making myself and a girl unhappy" says Kierkegaard through his narrator. (R, 115)

What then happens? The prodigy occurs. The hero breaks through to a new awareness in which he feels everything is restored. Kierkegaard coins a word for this new state: he calls it "repetition." At the time that he wrote *Fear and Trembling* and when he began *Repetition*, Kierkegaard himself apparently thought that what would be restored would be the thing that he loved most which he had given up (PK, 189). As Abraham had regained Isaac, Kierkegaard hoped to receive Regine back. During the course of the writing of *Repetition*, however, he received word that Regine had married another man. It was precisely in the anguish of this loss, Croxall notes, that Kierkegaard experienced his own "repetition" or new birth. (KS, 164)

Kierkegaard says that in the repetition one receives everything back double. What precisely then does he receive? The following makes it clear:

> His nature has become split, and so the quest is not about the repetition of something outward, but about the repetition of his freedom . . . Now providence intervenes with a helping hand . . . and then he bursts out with: "Is there not then a repetition? Did I not receive everything double? Did I not receive *myself* again, and precisely in such a way that I must feel doubly the significance of it? And in comparison with such a repetition, what is the repetition of earthly goods which for the spirit are indifferent?" (R, xxi).

Thus, when all seems lost, faith can break into the consciousness of the one who has entered on his quest. The knight of infinite resignation was brought to the point of losing "honor and pride, and along with that the will to live and the meaning of life" (R, 133). Repetition comes about "when all conceivable human certitude and probability pronounced it impossible" (Ibid.). By some act not his own there comes a relationship to God and hence to himself; only then can one return and live contentedly in what Percy calls "the ordinary lovely world."

Kierkegaard stresses that joy underlies the resignation and faith of the religious venture. "Hence the religious contradiction: at the same time to lie upon 70,000 fathoms of water and yet be joyful" (*SLW*, 430).

> I am again myself. This self which another would not pick up from the road I possess again. The discord in my nature is resolved, I am again unified. The terrors which found support in my pride no longer enter in to distract and separate. Is there not then a repetition? Did I not get everything doubly restored? Did I not get myself again, precisely in such a way that I must doubly feel its significance (*R*, 144)?

This fortunate one can return to live in the finite world based on a new relationship. In order to appreciate Kierkegaard's insight into what the new life of faith looks like one can do no better than to go to a description of it in his small volume, *Fear and Trembling*. In an unforgettable passage, he portrays a fictional being who embodies his important insight that "those who carry the jewel of faith are not so easily recognizable."

> Let me say frankly that I have never, in the course of my experience, seen a reliable example of the knight of faith, but I do not for a moment deny that every other man may be such a knight. Meanwhile I have spent years searching for him in vain. Men are accustomed to travelling the world, looking for rivers and mountains, new stars, birds of gay-coloured plumage, monstrous fishes, ridiculous races of men; they abandon themselves to an animal stupor and gaze open-mouthed at life, believing that they have seen something. None of these things interest me at all. But if I knew where there lived a single knight of faith, I would make a pilgrimage on foot to greet him; for this is the miracle which occupies my thoughts exclusively. Not for a moment would I let him out of my sight; I would watch how he performed each movement and consider myself made for life; I would divide my time between watching him and practising the movements he made, and thus spend all my time in admiring him. As I have said, I have never discovered a knight of the faith, but I can easily imagine one. Here he is. I make his acquaintance, I am introduced to him. And the moment I lay eyes on him, I push him away and leap back suddenly, clap my hands together and say half aloud: "Good God! Is this really he? Why,

he looks like an inspector of Taxes!" But it is really he. I draw closer to him, I watch every movement he makes to see whether he shows any sign of the least telegraphic communication with the infinite, a glance, a look, a gesture, an air of melancholy, a smile to betray the contrast of infinity and the finite. But no! I examine him from head to foot, hoping to discover a chink through which the infinite can peer through. But no! He is completely solid. How does he walk? Firmly. He belongs wholly to the finite; and there is no townsman dressed in his Sunday best, who spends his Sunday afternoon in Frederiksberg, who treads the earth more firmly then he; he belongs altogether to the earth, no bourgeois more so. In him you will find no trace of that exquisite exclusiveness which distinguishes the knight of the infinite. He takes pleasure in all things, takes part in everything, and everything he does, he does with the perseverance of earthly men whose souls hang fast to what they are doing. He does his job thoroughly. At first glance you would think he was a clerk who had lost his soul to double-entry bookkeeping, so punctilious he is. On Sundays he takes a holiday. He goes to church. No heavenly glance, no sign of incommensurability betrays him; and without knowing him it would be impossible to distinguish him from the rest of the congregation, for his healthy bellowing of the psalms proves only that he has got a sound pair of lungs. During the afternoons he walks out to the woods. His heart rejoices over everything he sees, the crowds, the new omnibuses, the Sound. If you met him on the *Strandvej*, you would think he was a shopkeeper having a good time, his delight being of that kind: for he is not a poet and I have tried in vain to detect in him any sign of poetic incommensurability. When he comes home in the evening, he walks as sturdily as a postman. On his way he thinks about the special hot dish which his wife has been preparing for him, a grilled lamb's head garnished with herbs perhaps. If he meets some one similarly disposed, he is quite capable of walking as far as Österport if only he can discuss the dish, and he will discuss it with a passion which would give credit to a *maître d'hôtel*. As it happens he has not fourpence to spare: but he still believes that his wife has a hot meal waiting for him. If she has, it will be an enviable sight for distinguished people and an inspiring one for common folk to see him eat; for his appetite is stronger than Esau's. If his wife has not prepared it, he remains—oddly enough—unmoved . . . In the evening he smokes his pipe, and to see him you would swear that he was the butcher from over the way, vegetating in the evening twilight. He is as free from cares as any ne'er-do-well, but every moment of his life he purchases his leisure at the highest price; for he makes not the least movement except by virtue of the absurd. And yet—and yet I could become furious at the thought of it, if only out of envy—this man is making and has made at every moment the movement of infinity! In infinite resignation he drains the dark waters of melancholy to the last drop; he knows the blessedness of infinity; he has known the pain of forsaking everything in the world that was most dear to him; and yet the taste of the finite is as pleasing to him as if he had never known anything higher, for he remains in the finite without betraying any sign of his uneasy and tortured training, and yet rejoices in it with so much assurance that for him there appears to be nothing more certain (*LTK*, 110–13).

The movement of faith, however, is never finished, warns Kierkegaard in *Stages*, "at least not in time and hence only as a delusion can it be so represented" (*SLW*, 403). It is true, he goes on, that "the religious sphere is that of fulfillment, but note, not such a fulfillment as when one fills a cane or a bag with gold." The greatest danger, he says, is not to discover that one is always in danger, "even if he had money and the handsomest girl and lovely children and was king of the land or one of the simplest folks free from all care." Although a basic characteristic of faith is joy, the question of where one finds the joy is all-important:

> The question is whether he has not been joyful in the wrong place. And where is the right place? It is . . . in danger above seventy thousand fathoms of water, many, many miles from all human help, there to be joyful—that is great! To swim in shallow water along with the bathers is not the religious. (Ibid., 425)

Kierkegaard warns repeatedly that religious existence "is never expressed by once in a while making a great effort, but by persistence in the relationship" (*CUP*, 476).

Thus we have Kierkegaard's expression of the characteristics of religious existence and how one may make the movement into it. Walker Percy has consciously portrayed in his contemporary fiction what Kierkegaard said he would gladly make a pilgrimage to see. Let us see what Percy shows us.

Chapter 9

Percy's Knights of Faith

In all of his fiction Walker Percy is concerned to show how the movement to recovered selfhood can be made. Even more pointedly than Kierkegaard, he sees it being made without necessarily involving conscious awareness of God. With the possible exception of Lancelot, each of his protagonists can be said to perform what Kierkegaard calls the "double movement of infinity." Will Barrett, the hero of both his second and his last novels, manifests it most clearly, and we shall see what his actions can tell us in each of the two stories. Thomas More, of *Love in the Ruins*, will be our other example. Tom's movement of infinite resignation takes a different form than Will's. We shall also observe his manner of life subsequent to making the "movement of faith," as it provides a contemporary image of the "knight of faith" strikingly similar to that provided by Kierkegaard.

THE YOUNGER WILL

Percy's portrayal of the movement from immediacy to faith does not stress the ethical as a separate stage, as does Kierkegaard's. Percy's protagonists make the break with immediacy by choosing despair, and immediately begin a search. The search, even though it is not explicitly motivated by a sense of God, is a response to an inner call and bears all the earmarks of the movement of resignation, the first movement of Kierkegaard's religious stage. It involves abstaining from "the customary ways of making do" and following a solitary path. It necessarily involves suffering because the "knight" puts aside normal life-supports in search of what can make his life possible. He is cut off from others, often misunderstood and sometimes even thought to be crazy. Percy says of the younger Will Barrett in the Ashley Brown interview:

> In the conventional view of things he's very sick. His symptoms of epilepsy, *déjà vu*, and so on. Binx is more relaxed . . . Barrett, on the other hand, has a *passionate pilgrimage* that he must follow, and he is looking for a father-figure. His symptoms are ambiguous, however, and he could go in various directions. The ambiguity is deliberate. The reader is free to see him as a sick man among healthy business men or as a sane pilgrim in a mad world (*Shen*, 7).

It will be recalled that the intensification of his despair in the fall of his junior year at Princeton was the catalyst that enabled Will to break with his dependent way of living and begin to act on his own. His search begins immediately. As he lives his solitary life in the Y.M.C.A. off Central Park his problem is, "how to live from one ordinary minute to the next on a Wednesday afternoon." The author is borrowing here from Kierkegaard and reflects in the next line: "Has not this been the case with all 'religious' people?" (*TLG*, 340). Will finds himself facing a maze of possibilities and has difficulty in deciding what to do with his life. "Golf he was good at, it was living that gave him trouble."

On his arrival in New York City, Will realized that two things were necessary as a start. "There was something the matter with him and it should be attended to. Treatment would take money and therefore he needed a job." He lost no time in putting himself in the hands of a psychiatrist whom he saw five days a week for the next five years. And, secondly, he enrolled in a six-month course to qualify for a $175 a week job as a maintenance engineer at Macy's, "really a kind of janitor."

That Will has begun the movement of resignation seems clear. He had responded to an inner necessity to leave the halls of Princeton where he felt so out of touch with himself. In so doing he has completely broken from what is expected of him. He moves to New York City, the other end of the world from his native Alabama. He immediately engages a psychiatrist and begins working as a janitor. A more radical resignation from a style of life congruent with his genteel Southern background can hardly be imagined. He does it all, however, with a sense of freedom and adventure as he sets out to find himself.

It may be seen that Will has suspended what Kierkegaard calls the "universal ethical requirement" in these activities. He has committed what is, in America, the unpardonable sin: he has turned his back on people. He realizes that he should be more sociable and even works on this with Dr. Gamow, his psychiatrist:

> He understood, moreover, that it is people who count, one's relations with people, one's warmth toward and understanding of people. At these times he set himself the goal and often achieved it of "cultivating rewarding interpersonal relationships with a variety of people"—to use a phrase he had come across and not forgotten. (Ibid., 11)

It does not work, however, because it is not enough for him; it is not the answer to his search, and he repeatedly finds himself moving away from people and onto his own solitary quest. In doing so he suffers from "fugue states," *déjà vus* and "*Lücken* or gaps." His psychiatrist sees him as a patient obsessed with "the great search for the 'answer' which will unlock everything."

Unfortunately, after five years with Dr. Gamow, Will finds that the analysis has not helped much. He has learned, for example, to adapt superficially to group relationships, but this has only taken him further away from himself:

> It is true that after several years of psychoanalysis and group therapy he had vastly improved his group skills. So thoroughly in fact did he identify with his group companions of the moment, so adept did he become at role-taking, as the social scientists call it, that he all but disappeared into the group. (Ibid., 19)

Will decides to break off his analysis. With this break, the first stage of his quest ends, and with little result.

However it is not long before things begin to move again. Simultaneously with stopping his analysis Will buys a telescope, and his quest enters a new phase. It is clear that the search is not a simple, planned course of action. It is a direction of life in which, if one persists, he may find . . . *himself*. When Will on one fateful morning looked through his telescope into Central Park there occurred "a chance event through which the rest of his life was to be changed."

> His heart gave a leap. He fell in love, at first sight and at a distance of two thousand feet. It was not so much her good looks . . . as a certain bemused and dry-eyed expression in which he seemed to recognize—himself! (Ibid., 7)

Thereafter, we are told, "he came to see that he was not destined to do everything but only one or two things. Lucky is the man who does not secretly believe that every possibility is open to him." So Will by "some dim dazzling trick of grace" moves a step forward in his search. (Ibid., 4)

We have already seen some of Will's subsequent involvement with Kitty's family, his friendship with Jamie and his pursuit of Sutter who he believes is "onto something." He has ventured out over Kierkegaard's 70,000 fathoms. He suffers the consequence of infinite resignation, the loss of the security of normal ways, friends, family, and prestige. He is painfully aware of the "gaps" in his psyche. But it is in this way alone, Percy insists, that he can find himself; that, to quote Kierkegaard, "Providence can get a grip on him."

It is only in such focussing of his attention that Will can advance on his quest. It requires a putting aside of other things. Percy's epigraph for *The Last Gentlemen* is Kierkegaard's observation that "If a man cannot forget he will never amount to much." Will is a forgetter of many things in his quest, and this is expressed metaphorically by presenting him as suffering from amnesia. Sutter explains Will's condition to him on one occasion:

> Look, Barrett, your trouble is due not to a disorder of your organism but to the human condition, that you do *well* to be afraid and you do *well* to forget everything which does not pertain to your salvation. That is to say, your amnesia is not a symptom. (Ibid., 339)

Percy may have in mind here another of Kierkegaard's observations on the same point in which the latter says: "Christianity requires Christians to forget something and in a certain sense to forget everything, to forget the multifarious" (*TIC*, 152). Will compared himself to Jamie who hoped to spend the next forty years "engrossed in an effort to add to 'science'." "The difference between me and him," thinks Will, "is that I could not permit myself to be so diverted (but diverted from what?)." (*TLG*, 231). He is resigned from the normal ways and is on a quest, but all is far from clear to him.

Kierkegaard insists that suffering is the primary characteristic of religious existence. Suffering is quite clearly central to Will's state. The suffering that results from his differentness from others is most immediately apparent. Consider his painful feeling of alienation from, and envy of the young men of his home Delta area, "Sewanee Episcopal types," who had come up for a college football game. They were:

> . . . . very much themselves with themselves, set, that is, for the next fifty years in the actuality of themselves and their own good names. They knew what they were, how things were and how things should be. As for the engineer, he didn't know. I'm from the Delta too, thought he, sticking his hand down through his pocket, and I'm Episcopal; why ain't I like them, easy and actual? Oh, to be like Rooney Lee. (Ibid., 255)

Will frequently has to stick his hand down through a hole in his pocket to hold down his knee which jumps convulsively in times of stress! The Sewanee Episcopal types had had everything easy and felt quite secure and confident in their privileged station. They had not yet allowed the negativities of life to enter their consciousness.

When Will had first returned from New York and resumed college in Alabama with Kitty and Jamie his suffering increased.

> The engineer, if the truth be told, was in a bad way, having been seriously dislocated by his first weeks at the university. . . . What had happened was that the university had badly thrown him off with its huge pleasantness. Powerful friendship radiations came at him from all directions. It was enough to make one uneasy. By ten o'clock on the first morning he was fairly jumping with nervousness. He did believe that the campus was the pleasantest place he had ever seen. Everyone he met was happy and good-looking and victorious and kindly and at-one with themselves, and here he was, solitary and goofy and shut up in himself, eyeballs rolled up in his eyebrows. (Ibid., 193–4)

Percy is, of course, clearly saying that Will's "sickness" is really his health because he has chosen the way that leads to self-integration. The happy, good-looking, victorious, kindly, and at-one-with themselves Episcopal Sewanee types on the other hand are the sick. They are those who, Kierkegaard says, are most in despair, being unaware of their despair. Will's suffering is further accentuated by the fact that he cannot explain himself to others. They would never understand what he meant by his search; they have never known there was anything that needed to be sought. He must therefore be silent as was Abraham.

> The Vaughts liked him fine of course, and did not notice that he was worse. For he was as prudent and affable as ever and mostly silent. (Ibid., 179)

Thus Will accepts the suffering described by Kierkegaard: "the suffering imposed for letting oneself be helped by Him, the punishment of being banished from the society of men" (*TIC*, 41).

The clearest single instance of resignation and suffering that we see in Will is his willingness to risk losing Kitty, his love, the one in whom he had recognized himself. In doing so in pursuit of his goal, he is again "suspending the ethical." Universally accepted standards of conduct would demand that he fulfill the obligation which he had undertaken in getting involved with her: get married and settle down. This he cannot do; his quest comes first.

What was wrong with a Mr. and Mrs. Williston Bibb Barrett living in a brand-new house in a brand-new suburb with a proper address: 2041 Country Club Drive, Druid Hills, Atlanta, Georgia?

Nothing was wrong, but he got worse anyway. This happiness of the South drove him wild with despair.

What was wrong with marrying him a wife, holding Kitty's charms in his arms the livelong night?

Nothing, but his memory deteriorated and he was assaulted by ghostly legions of *déjà vus* and often awoke not knowing where he was. His knee leapt like a fish. It became necessary to unravel the left pocket of his three pairs of pants in order to slip a hand down and keep his patella in place (*TLG*, 178–9).

We can see that Will is aided in this pursuit by something beyond his own powers—in this case the "gift" of his own disability, which gets worse when he considers abandoning his mission.

Finally the moment of choice comes.

"If they've gone to New Mexico, and I think they have, it'll take longer. I'll look in Santa Fe and Albuquerque. Kitty?" He waited in the doorway without looking at her.

When she did not move, he looked up. The girl was stricken. She was wringing the fingers of one hand. He had never seen anyone wring his hands.

"Are you coming with me?"

"I can't," she said, open-mouthed and soundless like a fourteen-year-old talking past the teacher.

"Why not?"

"Bill," said Rita, brow gone all quirky, "You can't ask this child to travel with you. Suppose you do have to go to New Mexico."

"We can be married in Louisiana tomorrow. My uncle lives there and can arrange it."

She [Rita] shook her head fondly.

Kitty is in Rita's power. It is elsewhere implied that Rita is sexually attracted to Kitty and wants Will out of the way so she can have her for herself. One can sense danger in the encounter, the presence of deceit and selfishness.

"She was daring him! If you leave, said the fine gray eyes, you know that I know you won't came back. I dare you!" (Ibid., 266)

In spite of this threat from his enemy, however, Will makes his decision and departs without his love.

"At its best," says the novelist Flannery O'Connor, "our age is an age of searchers and discoverers, and at its worst an age that has domesticated despair and learned to live with it happily." (*MM*, 159) Will is clearly one of Flannery O'Connor's best. He has all the earmarks of being a knight of infinite resignation. Let us see if he makes the second movement: the movement of faith.

WILL'S MOVEMENT OF FAITH

It may be well, as we inquire into whether the young Will Barrett makes the final movement of infinity, to be reminded of Kierkegaard's description of the knight of faith. He looks like anybody else with the one difference that he lives solidly in the world. He treads with a firm step and is interested in everything. He enjoys the simple pleasures of life, such as looking forward to the supper his wife will have prepared for him when he gets home. The definition of faith, says Kierkegaard, is that "by relating itself to its own self and by willing to be itself, the self is grounded transparently in the Power which constituted it" (*SD*, 262). So when a person by some miracle moves to a new inner relationship with its own self he finds himself able to live in the "ordinary lovely world," which he had to put aside in the first of the movements of infinity. Solidity is what Will has clearly lacked up to this point. Although he is able to see afresh and thus relate with others, his selfhood is described by the author as a "great sucking void of potentiality." He still does not know who he is and what he is to do and believes that the secret to unlock his life will have to come from outside, from Sutter. He is thus still dependent on something external, but of course, his basic need cannot be fulfilled in that way.

Let us see then what finally happens to Will. After he left Kitty with Rita he set out across country in the Trav-L-Aire, following certain clues left behind in Sutter's apartment, including a marked map and Sutter's casebook. He reads in the casebook from time to time on the journey and finds himself

more and more confused by what Sutter is saying. He finally
arrives in the small Arizona town where Sutter's clues have led
him. There he spends most of his time with Jamie until the boy
dies.

On one particular evening, back in his parked Trav-L-Aire,
Will reads the last of Sutter's casebook entries and finally
throws the casebook into the trashburner. In his loneliness and
dislocatedness "he became at once agitated and lustful." Then
he remembers that there was something in that last sentence
in the casebook that "had a bearing, it had read: 'I won't miss
next time' . . . "

> Jumping into the cab of the GMC he tore out of the poplar grove,
> forgetting his umbilical connections until he heard the snap-
> pings of cords and the shout of the Hoosier (*TLG*, 360).

He suddenly decides to stop and call Kitty, after which he races
out across the desert to the dude ranch, and to Sutter.

It is in this final major encounter with Sutter that something
decisive seems to take place within Will. He begins by asking
Sutter what it is that he wished to tell him, hoping that it will
be the answer he has been looking for. Sutter does not seem to
hear him but finally, when pressed, says he has nothing to tell
Will. A dialogue develops in which Sutter angrily says that
what was written in the casebook was not written for Will, and
anyway he no longer believes a word of it. They talk about Val
and her philosophy of "what God should be and what man is,
and even what the church should be." Sutter has essentially
given up on life: "When I first came to the desert I was waiting
for a sign, but there was no sign and I am not waiting for one
now." Will presses Sutter even further about what he has to
tell him and why he brought Jamie out to Arizona until finally,
in exasperation, "Sutter's feet hit the floor" and he explodes:
"Goddamn it Barrett what do you mean by requiring answers
from me? Why should I answer you? What are you to me?
Christ, if you recall I never solicited your company in the first
place." In spite of this outburst Will continues to press, even
going so far as to say that if Sutter would just tell him what to
do he would do it. Obviously he has not yet acquired his self!

There follows talk about Rita, about what Sutter will do, and about Will's decision to marry Kitty and "rejoin the human race." Finally, after Sutter tells him "Barrett, I think you'd better call the family" the following takes place in which, in Kierkegaard's metaphor, I belive the "thunderstorm breaks" for Will.

> "No, Barrett, I'll not be here."
>
> "Why not?" asked the other angrily—he had had enough of Sutter's defections.
>
> "Barrett," said Sutter as cheerfully as ever, craning his neck to keep track of the new guest, "if you know anything at all— and, what with your peculiar gifts, you know a good deal more than that—you ought to know why not."
>
> "I don't," said the engineer, at a total loss. He had lost his intuition!
>
> "If I do outlive Jamie," said Sutter, putting on his Curlee jacket (double breasted!), "it will not be by more than two hours. What in Christ's name do you think I'm doing out here? Do you think I'm staying? Do you think I'm going back?"
>
> The engineer opened his mouth but said nothing. For the first time in his life he was astonished.
>
> "You won't join me, Barrett?"
>
> "What? No. No, thanks."
>
> Sutter nodded cheerfully, dropped the pistol in the side pocket of the jacket, and hurried down the path after the last of the dudes.
>
> Perhaps this moment more than any other, the moment of his first astonishment, marked the beginning for the engineer of what is called a normal life. *From that moment forward it was possible to meet him and after a few minutes form a clear notion of what sort of fellow he was and how he would spend the rest of his life* (Ibid., 373–4, emphasis added).

Will had put everything else aside, including Kitty, his love, in order to pursue his passionate quest for what he needed to live by. Now, miraculously, his life is being enabled to begin as if for the first time. From the moment of his first astonishment he began to live as a definite someone, to know who he was and to be able to return and live "a normal life," no longer having to ask Sutter for answers or for instructions as to what to do. Will had often enough before resolved to overcome "the vacuum of his own potentiality" and become something definite, but without success. His old way is vividly described in the occasion just prior to his first meeting with Sutter when he had discovered that he could see him through a hole opening into the adjoining room.

> The old itch for omniscience came upon him—lost as he was in his own potentiality, having come home to the South only to discover that not even his own homelessness was at home here—but he resisted the impulse to eavesdrop. I will not overhear nor will I oversee, he said, and instead threw a dozen combination punches, for henceforth I shall be what I am no matter how potential I am. . . .
>
> He lay on the bed, feet sticking straight up, and broke into a cold sweat. What day is this, he wondered, what month, and he jumped up to get his Gulf calendar card from his wallet. The voices in the next room murmured away. A chair scraped back. The vacuum of his own potentially howled about him and sucked him toward the closet. He began to lean. Another few seconds, and he was holed up as snug as an Englishman in Somerset, closet door closed behind him, Val-Pak on his back like a chasable. (Ibid., 205)

Will, during that stage of his journey had experienced himself as a vacuum, a void. He knew that it was necessary for him to begin to be himself, to cease the life of the mere observer and responder, to cease, that is, the parasitic existence of "living on" others rather than out of himself. Although he had made the initial break with immediacy and was a concerned wayfarer, he continually lapsed away from himself and into an other-directed kind of immediacy. He threw a few combination punches to try to remind himself that he was something in himself—Look! I am and have been a fighter! It did not work however; his resolve always failed. "The vacuum of his own potentiality sucked him toward the closet door" and to the peephole. He finds himself again snug and safe in his hidden observation post in which someone *else* is his only reality. He had not yet made the second of the movements of infinity.

Now, however, in this final confrontation with Sutter, what he had not himself been able to achieve suddenly is his. "From that time forward it was possible to meet him and after a few minutes form a clear notion of what sort of fellow he was and how he would spend the rest of his life." He who had been lost is now found. He has been given *himself*, restored and reintegrated, which is what he needed all along. In Kierkegaard's terminology he experiences all the joy of having "received everything double"; he has received the true "repetition."

Although the change in Will came to full realization in this moment of recognition, it should not be supposed that it happened as an isolated event. It was preceded by a gradual, mainly subliminal, prehension on his part. For example, just prior to this he had already made a partial inner movement toward marriage. This was what he had talked about with Kitty on the phone and they had "settled a fair proportion" of things. However, until this final moment of new seeing, Will had still not been able to finalize the decision on his own. Before his breakthrough he tells Sutter of his tentative ideas, hanging as if for dear life on the latter's approval.

> "I think I'm going to be a pretty fair member of the community. God knows the place could use even a small contribution of good will and understanding."
> "Beyond a doubt. Good will and understanding. Yes. Very good."
> "Well?"
> "Well what?"
> "What's wrong with that?"
> "Nothing . . . "
> "I see. Dr. Vaught."
> "What?"
> "I know you think there is something wrong with it."
> "You do?"
> "Yes. I know you think there is everything wrong with it."
> (Ibid., 368–9)

After a few more vain attempts to convince Sutter, and thereby himself, that there is nothing wrong with it, he gives up and "gazes gloomily at the chuck wagon." *After* "the moment of his first astonishment," however, he no longer needs Sutter's approval.

What then has happened to Will? How has it happened and how can we understand it as a "movement of faith"? He has in some basic sense been restored to himself. A new inner relationship to himself has taken place which changes everything in his ability to live in the world. It is all right now for him to live as others do; he can accept it all, indeed rejoice in it. The dynamics of the movement are essentially those laid out by Kierkegaard in his discussion of what he calls "repetition." All along Will had searched for an answer, for some reality, beyond the here-and-now of the world around him. He had sought this, finally, in and through the person of Sutter. Gradually, however, through their meetings and through the casebook, it begins to appear that he will find no more from Sutter than he has through anything else. Finally, when inescapably faced with Sutter's utter void all seems lost. The one through whom Will had hoped to find out how to live tells him that he intends to kill himself in a matter of hours. Will's mouth drops open in astonishment. The thunderstorm of repetition breaks, for Kierkegaard, precisely when by human calculation all seems lost. (R, 133). It is not primarily that Will's understanding is enlightened, but that he receives what Kierkegaard calls an "existential communication" by which he is able to act (CUP, 342). What he receives is *himself*. The occasion for this is the sudden awareness that the other person in whom he had placed his hope has failed him. He then suddenly finds the power within himself. He discovers himself as a responsible being before God. He discovers, moreover, that he as an acting, responsible being has a fundamental responsibility for Sutter.

Another developing awareness helped prepare Will for this final breakthrough. This was the dim perception that the reality that he was looking for was not a spiritual abstraction "out there," but that it is intimately present in the concrete here and now. We see this on the occasion when Will stops by the family home where his aunts now live. He finds himself recalling his father's suicide. He recalls how his father had searched for reality in the spiritual, the music of Brahms, poetry, in his own solitary abstractive searching. Will, in the dark yard of the old home, touched "the tiny iron horsehead of the hitching post, traced the cold metal down to the place where the oak had grown around it in an elephant lip. His fingertips touched the warm finny whispering bark."

Wait. While his fingers explored the juncture of iron and bark, his eyes narrowed as if he caught a glimmer of light on the cold iron skull. *Wait.* I think he was wrong and that he was looking in the wrong place. No, not he but the times. The times were wrong and one looked in the wrong place. It wasn't even his fault because that was the way he was and the way the times were, and there was no other place a man could look. It was the worst of times, a time of fake beauty and fake victory. *Wait.* He had missed it! It was not in the Brahms that one looked and not in solitariness and not in the old sad poetry but—he wrung out his ear—*but here,* under your nose, here in the very curiousness and drollness and extraness of the iron and bark that—he shook his head—that—(*TLG,* 319).

Binx Bolling of *The Moviegoer* comes to the same awareness at the end of his own quest: "that God is himself present here at the corner of Elysian Fields and Bons Enfants" (*M,* 235).

Although God is not mentioned in the closing pages of *The Last Gentleman* what we see there in Will has all of the earmarks of what for Percy clearly marks the God-relationship. It exists when one has become aware of what Kierkegaard calls his own "eternal validity" that he *is* something in the universe and that something is expected of him. The requirement, in Percy's view, is that one is responsible to help meet the needs of those persons whose needs he sees and can do something about.

The new-found selfhood in Will can be seen clearly in the closing paragraph of the book. Jamie has died and Sutter has told Will that he is on his way back to the ranch. Will knows that he is going there with one intention in mind—to kill himself. The book closes with these words:

"Dr. Vaught, I want you to come back with me."

"Why? To make this contribution you speak of?"

"Dr. Vaught, I need you. I, Will Barrett—" and he actually pointed to himself lest there be a mistake, "—need you and want you to come back. I need you more than Jamie needed you. Jamie and Val too."

Sutter laughed. "You kill me, Barrett."

"Yes sir." He waited.

"I'll think about it . . . "

But as the Edsel took off, spavined and sprung, sunk at one

152

corner and flatulant in its muffler, spuriously elegant and un-
sound, like a Negro's car, a fake Ford, a final question did occur
to him and he took off after it.

"Wait," he shouted in a dead run.

The Edsel paused, sighed and stopped.

*Strength flowed like oil into his muscles and he ran with
great joyous ten-foot antelope bounds.*

The Edsel waited for him (*TLG*, 393, emphasis added).

Whether or not Percy intended "I, Will Barrett" to be taken as
a play on the words "I will bear it," such a word-play well expresses Will's new sense of himself. He will "bear" Sutter, take
responsibility insofar as he can for his staying alive. Having
been willing to suffer the movement of infinite resignation in
his passionate quest, he ends by receiving the one thing he
needs—the ability to will to be himself. In this, in Kierkegaard's phrase, he is "grounded transparently in God." Such
grounding does not necessarily mean that he is conscious of
God in any definite way. And this too is good news for modern
man who in great measure seems, at least for the time being,
to have lost that very ability.

THOMAS MORE

Dr. Tom More, the hero of *Love in the Ruins*, provides further
insights into how one can move into selfhood and what that
is like. His movement of infinite resignation has a different
dimension from that of the young Will Barrett. Whereas Will's
passionate quest is concerned directly with finding the one
great answer and purpose for himself, Tom's is focussed on
finding a way to cure mankind whose selfhood is "rendered
from itself." For this purpose he is willing to suffer.

Dr. Thomas More is a "somewhat shaky psychiatrist" in his
early fifties. The author uses allegorical imagery to portray the
radical dimensions of the divided human state and the pos-
sibilites of a cure. The story is about the impending final days
of the earth: a catastrophe is immanent because man's "lapsed"
condition has advanced to the flash point, both in the individual and in society. The opening lines of the book set the
stage:

NOW IN THESE DREAD LATTER DAYS of the old violent beloved U.S.A. and of the Christ-forgetting Christ-haunted death-dealing Western world I came to myself in a grove of young pines and the question came to me: has it happened at last?

Two more hours should tell the story. One way or the other. Either I am right and a catastrophe will occur, or it won't and I'm crazy. In either case the outlook is not so good.

Here I sit, in any case, against a young pine, broken out in hives and waiting for the end of the world (*LIR*, 3).

Tom More, like the prescient engineer of the earlier novel, is the only one who can see afresh. He is a see-er into the culture, like the prophets of old. The danger is portrayed allegorically as being of an external and physical nature—a chemical reaction and fallout—but its effects are interior to man.

> These are bad times.
> Principalities and powers are everywhere victorious. Wickedness flourishes in high places.
> There is a clearer and more present danger, however. For I have reason to believe that within the next two hours an unprecedented fallout of noxious particles will settle hereabouts and perhaps in other places as well. It is a catastrophe whose cause and effects—and prevention—are known only to me. The effects of the evil particles are psychic rather than physical. They do not burn the skin and rot the marrow; rather do they inflame and worsen the secret ills of the spirit and rive the very self from itself. (Ibid., 5)

It is soon clear in the story that the divided state of man is the same as Percy has shown us before—the tendency to evade one's sovereign selfhood by falling into either abstraction or sensuality, angelism or bestialism. Percy provided a preview for this novel in an article entitled "Notes for a Novel About the End of the World" which appeared in the religious journal *Katallagete* shortly before the book itself appeared. In this article he set forth his thesis that man's consciousness in these modern times is in a most unhealthy condition and the individual "needs to come to himself through some such catalyst as catastrophe or ordeal" and to recover himself "as neither angel nor organism but as a wayfaring creature somewhere between." (*K*, 10) Gabriel Marcel predicts that some great catastrophe is inevitable for modern man unless the pervading "spirit of abstraction" which cuts the self off from the living roots of life and relationship can be halted (*CF*, 10).

The spirit of abstraction means such things as living by ideologies instead of by the facts, treating people as statistics or categories rather than as persons, and mouthing clichés instead of saying what one really thinks. In this novel the society of the new-old south has become polarized. The rightist Knotheads and the leftist Leftpapas can no longer speak to each other; the blacks, known as the Bantus, are in open rebellion; young people have dropped out in large numbers and are living as "love couples" in the swamp (*LIR*, 17). Even the Roman Catholic Church has fragmented into three competing groups. Elderly people are conditioned to adapt happily to a life of institutional care in Geriatrics Rehabilitation, or "Gerry Rehab," by the use of the "Skinner box." If they do not accept this, they can be shipped off to the "Happy Isles Separation Center," the euthanasists' pride and joy, where they are conditioned to pull their own "Euphoric Switch." Dr. More's professional-class neighbors in comfortable "Paradise Estates" are largely oblivious of the deterioration of society going on around them. They enjoy their country club, golf tournaments, and their "Bible Brunch" where they honor "Jesus Christ, the Greatest Pro of Them All." (Ibid., 83)

In this situation Thomas More performs the creative and continuing act of seeing the dread state of man's brokenness and acting on an idea which he hopes may lead to a cure. In the eyes of his colleagues he is slightly mad, but harmlessly so. In any event, he is not taken seriously. Out of an experience of deep personal tragedy, Tom has come to himself as a "wayfarer" with a mission beyond that of merely adapting to life. It is his willingness to see and to act upon what he sees, and his valiant suffering in this persevering action which constitute his movement of infinite resignation.

The thing that strikes the reader most emphatically is Tom's essential aloneness as he pursues his task. He alone sees the danger and he alone has an idea as to how to deal with it. Since the others can see no real problem Tom is totally unable to convince them of what he is about. They politely change the subject: "But when I called his attention to the vines cracking his slab, he seemed not to hear and instead showed me his mower." (Ibid., 10) The ubiquitous vines growing through the cracks in the roads and sidewalks symbolize the deterioration in society.

Tom's invention, which he hopes will be the key to curing man's "riven" state, is a device he calls a "lapsometer." "Only in man does the self miss itself, fall from itself (hence lapsometer!)."

> Suppose—! Suppose I could hit upon the right dosage and weld the broken self whole! What if a man could reenter paradise, so to speak, and live there both as man and spirit, whole and intact man-spirit, as solid flesh as a speckled trout, a dappled thing, yet aware of itself as a self! (*LIR*, 36).

Like all of Percy's protagonists, Tom had been enabled before the narrative began to make the break from immediacy and into seeing on his own through a personal catastrophe. His beloved twelve-year-old daughter had died of a neuroblastoma and his wife, Doris, had subsequently left him. His earlier promise as a medical researcher seemed premature.

> Alas, the promise didn't pan out. On the contrary. There followed twenty years of silence and decline. My daughter, Samantha died; my wife ran off with a heathen Englishman—come to think of it, I haven't seen a Christian Englishman for years—and I left off research, left off eating Christ in Communion, and took to sipping Early Times instead and seeking the company of the fair sex, as they used to say. (Ibid., 24)

Tom sometimes wonders if Samantha's death had broken his heart. However, after a while he discovered that "the period of my decline was also a period of lying fallow and of the germination of some strange quirky ideas."

> It happened while I was ill.
> One stormy night I lay in a hospital bed recovering from seizures of alternating terror and delight with intervening periods of immense longing. These attacks are followed in my case by periods of extraordinary tranquility of mind, of height-

ened perception, clairvoyance, and increased inductive powers.
. . . Then it was that my great idea came to me. So confident was
I of its value that I leapt out of bed at the height of the storm
and yelled to my fellow patients:

"Don't be afraid, brothers! Don't cry! Don't tremble! I have
made a discovery that will cure you! Believe me, brothers!"

"We believe you, Doc!" the madmen cried in the crashing
thunder, and they did. Madmen, like possessed souls in the
Gospels, know when you are telling the truth.

It was my fellow physicians who gave me trouble (Ibid. 28).

So, again, through the catalyst of despair, Tom finds what he
is to do, becomes aware of a demand laid upon him alone. In
response to this we see him in the story giving his all to the
task of developing his discovery for the good of his fellows—
and being considered mad for his trouble.

As a knight of infinite resignation Tom is first of all detached
from the ordinary ways in which people get along:

Who am I? You might well wonder. Let me give a little
dossier.

I am a physician, a not very successful psychiatrist; an alco-
holic, a shaky middle-aged man subject to depressions and ela-
tions and morning terrors, but a genius nevertheless who sees
into the hidden causes of things and erects simple hypotheses
to account for the glut of everyday events. . . .

My afflictions attract some patients, repel others. People are
generally tolerant. Some patients, knowing my frailties,
calculate I'll understand theirs. (Ibid., 11)

A little later he says of himself "I am possessed by terror and
desire and live a solitary life." Tom's solitariness pervades the
story. Most of the time he is occupied with his own thoughts
as, in the four-day span of the narrative, he quietly and per-
sistently goes about his task of making his lapsometer an effec-
tive instrument to heal people. Basic to his task is his need to
observe what is going on, to "watch and listen."

The author and critic Alfred Kazin, describing Percy in an article, could have been describing any of Percy's protagonists:
"The mental refusal, the silent spiritual opposition, the effort
to make some countervailing gesture are those of a man who
seems to be *here*, with us, but is really out *there*, all by him-

self." (HAR, 85) Tom has to leave other desirable activities to do what he sees he must do. He is quite attracted to the opposite sex and there are three young ladies with whom he is involved. However, we see him on numerous occasions acting in accordance with what he said once when one of these companions was appealingly present: "I have other fish to fry."

A final example of Tom's differentness can be seen in an amusing observation he makes as he takes cover in his house when the danger outside, real or imaginary, is increasing.

> Here is the "hunt" room, Doris's idea, fitted out with gun cabinet, copper sink, bar, freezer, billiard table, lifesize stereo-V, easy chairs, Audubon prints. Doris envisioned me coming here after epic hunts with hale hunting companions eviscerating the bloody little carcasses of birds in the sink, pouring sixteen-year-old bourbon in the heavy Abercrombie field-and-stream glasses and settling down with my pipe and friends and my pointer bitch for a long winter evening of man talk and football-watching. Of course I never came here, never owned a pointer bitch, had no use for friends, and instead of hunting took to hanging around Paradise Bowling Lanes and drinking Dixie beer with my partner, Leroy Ledbetter (LIR, 269–70).

Tom's resignation from the mainstream is manifested in yet other ways. It is clearly present in his willingness to sacrifice the high opinion of others, which he would have had as a "normal" doctor, in pursuit of his mission. He is willing to appear to others as slightly "off", as sick and weak. For example, in seeing people as persons rather than as types, Tom is moved to accept them as patients when other doctors would not.

> Late last night a love couple crept out of the swamp and appeared in my "enclosed patio." This often happens. Even though I am a psychiatrist, denizens of the swamp appear at all hours suffering from malaria, dengue, flukes, bummers, hepatitis, and simple starvation. Nobody else will treat them. (Ibid., 46)

Victor, a local black man, explains to Uru, the northern Negro who has come in to organize the black takeover: "Doc here the onliest one come to your house when you're sick. He sit up all one night with my auntee." Charlie Parker, the Paradise golf pro, says to Tom: "What you need is eighteen every night under the lights, like the other docs." But, of course, Tom is not like the other docs.

In a humorous scene, which reveals a great deal about where Tom is and where his colleagues are in their respective life-stances, the hero moves cautiously along the deserted golf course taking cover occasionally to avoid the danger which he alone sees. Suddenly—

> A crashing in the vines ahead of me. My heart stops: if it is a sniper, there's an army of them. Wait. Yes, whew. I spot Colley's pith helmet and Gottlieb's fishing cap. It is the Audubon Society, on the trail of the lordly ivorybill. (Ibid., 99)

In this, as in many other instances, Tom is presented as pursuing his purpose to try to perfect a device for healing man's self-alienated condition and putting everything else second to this task. His colleagues meanwhile find ways to pass their time in aesthetic enjoyment—birdwatching!

Tom's suffering in giving himself to his task occasionally becomes acute. At times his inner stress and the lack of understanding from others leads to periods of confinement in the hospital mental ward.

> "No fanks."
> "What? Oh. Then I'll see you shortly."
> " Fime."
> I do not speak well. I've lost. I'm a patient. But Buddy doesn't notice . . .
> "We can go now," whispers Moira. She sees the abyss and is willing to save me.
> "When will you come in?" asks Buddy.
> "Eins upon a oncy," I reply.
> "O.K. *Eins zwei drei*," says Buddy, willing to give me the benefit of the doubt. (Ibid., 208)

As he tries to tell his doctor colleagues what he sees as man's problem he meets the same kind of incomprehension often met by the person of religious faith. "Well, now. The soul of Western man," says Max, "that's a large order, Tom. Besides being rather uh metaphysical." (Ibid., 115)

There is an aspect of Tom's life-style at this point which points up one's limitations even when making the movements of infinity. We might suppose, in light of all that has been said, that Tom is all business and no pleasure. This is not the case at all. In fact, a great deal of Tom's time in the story is spent in making arrangements for secret trysts with his three lady loves. He arranges separate motel rooms in the same abandoned Howard Johnson motel for this purpose! Furthermore, Tom never lets himself get too far from his sip of Early Times or his favorite breakfast drink of Tang, duck eggs, and gin. One of his pastimes is to sit in his enclosed patio, listen to *Don Giovanni*, the opera that epitomized sensuous immediacy for Kierkegaard, and sip his toddies. Art Immelmann, the devil figure in the story, had shown Tom how his lapsometer could be used to stimulate the sensuous areas of the brain. After this, when things became tense, Tom would "take a small knock of Early Times and administer a plus-four sodium jolt to Brodmann 11, the zone of the musical-erotic."

How can these aesthetic delights be seen as not conflicting with the religious movement of resignation? The answer is that these activities do not dominate Tom; his central purpose always comes first. As Kierkegaard observed: "The aesthetic is not demolished, it is only dethroned." Tom's priorities are typically indicated in the following exchange.

> "O.K. Lola will do for you. We'll work in the garden, and in the evenings we'll sit here and drink and play music and watch the mad world go by. How does that sound?"'
>
> "Fine," I say, pleased despite myself at the prospect of spending the evening so, sipping toddies here in the swing while Lola plays Dvořák, clasping the cello between her noble knees.
>
> "Tom Tom singing to Lola?" she asks and I become aware I am humming "Là ci darem" from *Don Giovanni*. My musical-erotic area, Brodmann 11, is still singing like a bird.
>
> I pick up the 30.06. *"There's something I have to take care of first"* (Ibid., 280, emphasis added).

What Tom has to do first, of course, concerns his central task of healing people's riven psyches with his lapsometer in order to head off the impending disaster.

This does not mean that the author sees the aesthetic as

merely harmless. Art, the devil figure, holds it out to Tom precisely to tempt him from this purpose. Art says to Tom:

> "So that in the same moment one becomes victorious in science one also becomes victorious in love. And all for the good of mankind! Science to help all men and a happy joyous love to help women. We are speaking here of happiness, joy, music, spontaneity, you understand. Fortunately we have put behind us such unhappy things as pure versus impure love, sin versus virtue, and so forth. This love has its counterpart in scientific knowledge: it is neutral morally, abstractive and godlike—"
>
> "Godlike?"
>
> "In the sense of being like a god in one's freedom and omniscience." (Ibid., 213–4)

Percy portrays Tom, however, as using his bourbon and his female companions not as a diversion from his purpose but almost as a needed aid to facilitate its achievement.

Tom's movement to faith reveals the same basic ingredients as does that of Will Barrett. He suffers despair at losing all when the lapsometer falls into the devil's hands and the catastrophe occurs, complete with burning sand pits symbolizing hell. But as he stands, resisting to the end the devil's attempts to lure him to Copenhagen to receive the Nobel prize for his invention, finally the "thunderstorm breaks" and he receives himself back whole. After this he no longer needs his Early Times and his three lady friends. He marries one of them who has proven his staunch companion and defender, Ellen Oglethorpe, his office nurse.

Percy's portrayal of Tom five years later, after the decisive second movement, enables us to see what the author envisions as the goal of living, for which everyone should strive. What we see, is a man who is content, who is open to and receiving from the richness of what Percy is wont to call "the ordinary lovely world." The final chapter, entitled "Five Years Later," opens as follows:

> Hoeing collards in my kitchen garden. A fine December day. It is cold but the winter sun pours into the walled garden and fills it up.
>
> After hoeing a row: sit in the sunny corner, stretch out my

legs and look at my boots. A splendid pair of new boots of soft oiled leather, good for hunting and fishing and walking to town. For the first time I understand what the Confederate soldier was always saying: a good pair of boots is the best thing a man can have.

A poor man sets store by good boots. Ellen and I are poor. We live with our children in the old Quarters. Constructed of slave brick worn porous and rounded at the corners like sponges, the apartments are suprisingly warm in the winter, cool in summer. They are built like an English charterhouse, a hundred apartments in a row along the bayou, each with a porch, living room or (in my case) library, two bedrooms, kitchen, garden, one behind the other.

Waiting and listening and looking at my boots.

Here's one difference between this age and the last. Now while you work, you also watch and listen and wait. In the last age we planned projects and cast ahead of ourselves. We set out to "reach goals." We listened to the minutes of the previous meeting. Between times we took vacations. (Ibid., 381–2)

The similarity in life-tone between Tom and Kierkegaard's knight of faith who "takes delight in everything . . . tends to his work . . . and looks like any other man" is unmistakable (*FT*, 50). Tom is quite a different person from what he was when he was on his passionate quest. He has recovered himself as the result of the pursuit of his mission, and he is, for the first time, able to enjoy the simple things of life. He is living in what Kierkegaard calls "the second immediacy"; that is, he can live as a joyous recipient of life after the completion of his struggles in infinite resignation. He lives in a mode in which "while you work, you also watch and listen and wait." He has, by some miracle, moved into what the author calls "the spirit of the new age of watching and waiting." (*LIR*, 387). Having become related in a new way to himself he is "grounded transparently in the Power which constituted him" (*SD*, 262).

What, then, do we now see in Tom? First of all, it is abundantly clear that he takes delight in everything:

Through the open doorway I can see Ellen standing at the stove in a swatch of sunlight. She stirs grits. Light and air flow around her arm like the arm of Velasquez's weaver girl. Her half apron is lashed just above the slight swell of her abdomen.

She socks spoon down on pot and cocks her head to listen for the children, slanting her dark straight eyebrows. A kingfisher goes ringing down the bayou.

Meg and Thomas More, Jr., are still asleep.

Chinaberries bounce off the tin roof.

The bricks are growing warm at my back. In the corner of the wall a garden spider pumps its web back and forth like a child on a swing (*LIR*, 382).

He goes on to reflect upon the fact that his "practice is small. But my health is better." He gets up every morning at six to run his trotline across the bayou:

Water is the difference! Water is the mystical element! At dawn the black bayou breathes a white vapor. The oars knock, cypress against cypress, but the sound is muffled, wrapped in cotton. As the trotline is handed along, the bank quickly disappears and the skiff seems to lift and be suspended in a new element globy and white. Silence presses in and up from the vaporish depths come floating great turtles, blue catfish, lordly gaspergous. (Ibid., 383)

Second, Tom experiences himself as a sovereign being living from within himself and no longer in bondage to external influences and desires.

Strange: I am older, yet there seems to be more time, time for watching and waiting and thinking and working. All any man needs is time and desire and the sense of his own sovereignty. As Kingfish Huey Long used to say: every man is a king. I am a poor man but a kingly one. If you want and wait and work, you can have. (Ibid., 382)

Tom has wanted and pursued, and now he has. "Faith," says Kierkegaard, "is a miracle, and yet no man is excluded from it" (*FT*, 77). Tom says, "What I want is no longer the Nobel, screw prizes, but just to figure out what I've hit on—"

Some day a man will walk into my office as ghost or beast or ghost-beast and walk out as a man, which is to say sovereign wanderer, lordly exile, worker and waiter and watcher (*LIR*, 383).

This is exactly what he, in fact, has finally become. In his new age, he has lost his desire for honors and prestige. He has been excluded by the local Bantu medical society so he cannot use the hospital in spite of the fact that he is known as "a marvelous diagnostician." A doctor friend says to him "Rest assured, however, some of us are working on it." Tom simply responds, "All right," and lets it go. He makes ends meet by moonlighting with a fat clinic! "At noon today, in fact, I meet with my fat ladies at the Bantu Country Club." The black Bantus have taken over and now make up 99 percent of Paradise Estates. It is clear that Tom's new condition is one in which he is not at all bothered by what others might feel as putdowns. He has all the gratification he needs.

The third thing to be noticed is that Tom is still not immune from illicit desires of the flesh! As Martin Luther insisted, every man of faith is still a sinner. On Christmas Eve, the day in which the five-years-later scene is set, he goes to confession for the first time in eleven years and confesses to his friend, Father Smith, that even though he is a husband and a father "that does not prevent me from desiring other women and even contriving plans to commit fornication and adultery." He accuses himself of "drunkenness, lusts, envies, fornication, delight in the misfortunes of others, and loving myself better than God and other men." He admits that he cannot even genuinely feel sorry for this, but that he has not actually committed fornication and adultery recently. Father Smith reminds him that there are things we must think about: "like doing our jobs, you being a better doctor, I being a better priest, showing a bit of ordinary kindness to people, particularly our own families—unkindness to those close to us is such a pitiful thing . . ." "You're right. I'm sorry," says Tom, instantly chastened. (Ibid., 398–9)

The final thing to be observed in Tom is his new state of marriage, his new joy in having only one wife and needing only one: "Only one woman to my name now, a lusty tart Presbyterian, but one is enough." Tom has ordered for Ellen's Christmas present "a brass bed, king-size (60") with nonallergenic Posture-mate mattress and serofoam polyurethane foundation,

Sears best. The whole works: $603.95. A year's savings went into it mainly from my fat clinic." Tom's devotion to his "only one woman" is amply reflected here. Though poor, he has given her a wonderful gift indeed! And he goes to great pains to get it into the house without her seeing it.

Tom's new attitude toward other women can be seen in an encounter on the same Christmas Eve with Mrs. Prouty, his "good-humored thirty-five year old neighbor." "Whenever she used to see me buying a bottle next door at the Little Napoleon she'd say: 'Somebody's going to have a party. Can I come?' " Mrs. Prouty works at Sears in catalogue sales, and when Tom ordered his new Christmas boots she said, " 'These can go under mine any day,' merry eye roving past me carelessly."

> "Ma'am? Eh? Right! Har har!"
> These = my boots?
> Mine = her bed?
> Nowadays when a good-looking woman flirts with me, however idly, I guffaw like some ruddy English lord, haw, haw har, har harr harr. (Ibid., 392)

In the final scene of the book we find Tom on Christmas Day "Barbecuing in my sackcloth," which Father Smith has given him as a symbol of his confession and repentence.

> I'm dancing around to keep warm, hands in pockets. It is Christmas Day and the Lord is here, a holy night and surely that is all one needs.
> On the other hand I want a drink. Fetching the Early Times from a clump of palmetto, I take six drinks in six minutes. Now I'm dancing and singing old Sinatra songs and the *Salve Regina*, cutting the fool like David before the ark or like Walter Huston doing a jig when he struck it rich in the Sierra Madre.
> The turkey is ready. I take it into the kitchen and grab Ellen from behind. She smells of flour and stuffing and like a Georgia girl.
> "Oh, for pity's sake," says Ellen, picking up a spoon. (Ibid., 402)

Tom picks Ellen up, "a noble, surprisingly heavy, Presbyterian armful," and carries her off to her new $600 bed.

To bed we go for a long winter's nap, twined about each other as the ivy twineth, not under a bush or in a car or on the floor or any such humbug as marked the past peculiar years of Christendom, but at home in bed where all good folk belong.

It can be seen that the marks of Tom's new age are quite conservative in style. One must agree, however, that if he is a representative example of that "new age," no greater joy could be asked.

Chapter 10

Epilogue

S⌀ren Kierkegaard saw the most serious threat to human existence as being what he called "the sickness unto death," which results from a person's failing to live his or her life. He believed the cure for that sickness was continually offered to each individual through the very process of life itself, in which one is offered the opportunities and the power to make choices that will lead to self-recovery. Self-recovery consists in finally coming to the point at which the self is able "to relate itself to its own self and is willing to be itself." It is then "grounded transparently in the Power that constituted it." It has become concrete as a self. This, as has been noted, is what Kierkegaard calls the definition of faith (*SD*, 262). The Power that works through the processes of life is what enables the choice, but it is the *individual* who must choose if he or she is to make the movements to faith.

The great contribution of both Kierkegaard and Percy to our troubled age, in which traditional understanding of the wellsprings of life is weakening, is to point to certain processes as the means through which persons move to selfhood. With traditional religion losing its power, the insights of these two thinkers may be of vital importance. They are saying that apart from religion and even apart from conscious awareness of transcendence, God is present in life's process, providing the means for the movement of faith. It is a matter of existential choice for the individual, but the choice is made possible by

God. And the specific catalyst for such choice is, strangely enough, the very sense of despair that one normally tries to evade.

All of this, of course, means that persons who seem to have no operative thought of God are, in fact, every day making movements toward selfhood or are failing to. If Kierkegaard and Percy are correct in what they see, most people are failing to; perhaps they are overly pessimistic in their assessment of what actuates the majority of people. In any case, they both believe in a God who never ceases building the fires that enable the choice for life. If this God never ceases his curative action, then who can say that anyone will be able to withstand his love through all eternity?

In Percy's most recent novel, the elder Will Barrett has reached the joy of relating himself to himself, willing to be himself after a tumultous journey to this point. He begins to get a glimpse of the Power in whom he is transparently grounded as being present in and through both the terrible trials and the faithful persons that life has given him. The book ends with the following image of hope for all of Will Barrett's fellow wayfarers:

> Will Barrett stopped the old priest at the door and gazed into his face. The bad eye spun and the good eye looked back at him fearfully: What do you want of me? What do I want of him, mused Will Barrett, and suddenly realized he has gripped the old man's wrists as if he were a child. The bones were like dry sticks. He let go and fell back. For some reason the old man did not move but looked at him with a new odd expression. Will Barrett thought about Allie in her greenhouse, her wide gray eyes, her lean muscled boy's arms, her strong quick hands. His heart leapt with a secret joy. What is it I want from her and him, he wondered, not only want but must have? Is she a gift and therefore a sign of a giver? Could it be that the Lord is here, masquerading behind this simple silly holy face? Am I crazy to want both, her and Him? No, not want, must have. And will have (SC, 360).

Bibliography

ABBREVIATIONS OF SOURCES FOR NOTES

AMER   Percy, Walker. "The Coming Crisis in Psychiatry." *America*, XCVI (January, 1957), 391-93; 415-18.

Attack   Kierkegaard, Søren. *Attack Upon Christendom*. Translated by Walter Lowrie. Boston: Beacon Press, 1944.

CD   _____. *The Concept of Dread*. Translated by Walter Lowrie. Princeton: Princeton University Press, 1957.

CF   Marcel, Gabriel. *Creative Fidelity*. Translated by Robert Rosthal. New York: Noonday Press, a division of Farrar, Straus and Giroux, 1964.

CL   Kierkegaard, Søren. *Consider the Lilies*. Translated by A. S. Aldworth and W. S. Ferrie. London: C. W. Daniel Co., Ltd., 1940.

COMM   Baum, Gregory. Commonweal XCIV (May 28, 1971) 294.

CUP   _____. *Concluding Unscientific Postscript*. Translated by David F. Swenson and Walter Lowrie. Princeton: Princeton University Press, 1941.

ED   _____. *Edifying Discourses*. Translated by David F. Swenson and Lillian Marvin Swenson. 2 vols. Minneapolis: Augsburg Publishing House, 1962.

E/O   _____. *Either/Or*. Translated by David F. Swenson and Lillian Marvin Swenson with revisions by Howard A. Johnson. 2 vols. New York: Doubleday & Company, Inc., 1959.

169

170

FT   _____. *Fear and Trembling and The Sickness Unto Death*. Translated by Walter Lowrie. Princeton: Princeton University Press, 1954.

FOR   Percy, Walker. "The Act of Naming." *Forum*, II (Summer, 1958), 4–9.

GR   Carr, John. "An Interview with Walker Percy," *The Georgia Review*, XXV, No. 3, Fall 1971.

HAR   Kazin, Alfred. "The Pilgrimage of Walker Percy." *Harper's* CCXLII (June 1971), 81-86.

JD   Kierkegaard, Søren. *The Journals of Søren Kierkegaard*. Edited and translated by Alexander Dru. London, New York, Toronto: Geoffrey Cumberlage, Oxford University Press, 1951.

JH   _____. *Søren Kierkegaard's Journals and Papers*. Edited and translated by Howard V. Hong and Edna H. Hong. 2 vols. Bloomington: Indiana University Press, 1967—.

K   Percy, Walker. "Notes for a Novel about the End of the World." *Katallagete*, III (Fall, 1970), 5–12.

KC   Croxall, T. H. *Kierkegaard Commentary*.

KCEP   Wild, John. "Kierkegaard and Contemporary Existentialist Philosophy."

KP   Swenson, David F. *Kierkegaardian Philosophy in the Faith of a Scholar*.

KS   Croxall, T. H. *Kierkegaard Studies*.

L   _____. *Lancelot*. New York: Farrar, Straus and Giroux, 1977.

LTK   Auden, W. H., ed. *Living Thoughts of Kierkegaard*.

LIR   _____. *Love in the Ruins*. New York: Farrar, Straus and Giroux, 1971.

M   _____. *The Moviegoer*. New York: Noonday Press, a division of Farrar, Straus and Giroux, 1961.

MA   May, Rollo. *The Meaning of Anxiety*.

MB   _____. *The Message in the Bottle*. New York: Farrar, Straus and Giroux, 1975.

MM   O'Connor, Flannery. *Mystery and Manners*.

PERS   _____. "Naming and Being." *Personalist*, XLI (Spring, 1960), 148-57.

PH   Kierkegaard, Søren. *Purity of Heart Is To Will One Thing*. Translated by Douglas V. Steere. New York and London: Harper & Brothers Publishers, 1938.

PK   _____. *The Prayers of Kierkegaard.* Edited by Perry
            D. LeFevre. Chicago: University of Chicago Press,
            1956.

PPR   Percy, Walker. "Symbol as Hermeneutic in Existen-
            tialism." *Philosophy and Phenomenological
            Research,* XVI (1956), 522–30.

PV   Kierkegaard, Søren. *The Point of View for My Work as an
            Author.* Translated by Walter Lowrie. Edited by Ben-
            jamin Nelson. New York: Harper & Row,
            Publishers, 1962.

R   _____. *Repetition.* Translated by Walter Lowrie.
            Princeton: Princeton University Press, 1941.

REN   Henisey, Sarah. "Intersubjectivity and Symbolization."
            Renascence, XX (Summer, 1968), 208–14.

SHEN   Brown, Ashley. "An Interview with Walker Percy."
            Shenandoah, XVIII (Spring, 1967), 4–10.

SC   Percy, Walker. *The Second Coming.* New York: Farrar,
            Straus and Giroux, 1980.

SD   See FT.

SK   Rohde, Peter. *Søren Kierkegaard.* Translated by Alan
            Moray Williams. London: George Allen & Unwin
            Ltd., 1963.

SLW   Kierkegaard, Søren. *Stages on Life's Way.* Translated by
            Walter Lowrie. New York: Schocken Books, 1967.

TLG   Percy, Walker. *The Last Gentleman.* New York: Farrar,
            Straus and Giroux, 1966.

WPG   Douglas, Ellen. *Walker Percy's The Last Gentleman.* New
            York: Seabury Press, 1969.

OTHER SOURCES

Auden, W.H., ed. *The Living Thoughts of Kierkegaard.* Bloomington:
    Indiana University Press, 1952.
_____. "For the Time Being." *The Collected Poetry of W. H.
    Auden.* New York: Random House, 1945.
Aulén, Gustaf. *The Faith of the Christian Church.* Translated by Eric
    H. Wahlstrom and G. Everett Arden. Philadelphia: Muhlenburg
    Press, 1948.
"Authors that Bloom in the Spring." *Publishers' Weekly,* CXCIX
    (March 22, 1971), 23–24.

Baum, Gregory. Letter to the Editor. *Commonweal*, XCIV (May 28, 1971), 294.

Bradbury, John M. "Absurd Insurrection: The Barth-Percy Affair." *South Atlantic Quarterly,*, LXVIII (Summer, 1969), 319–29.

Catinella, Joseph. "Love in the Ruins" (review). *Saturday Review*, May 15, 1971, pp. 42–43.

Collins, James. *The Mind of Kierkegaard*. Chicago: Henry Regnery Company, 1953.

Croxall, T. H. *Kierkegaard Commentary*. New York: Harper and Brothers Publishers, 1956.

_____. *Kierkegaard Studies*. New York: Harper & Bros., 1958.

Duffy, Martha. "Lapsometer Legend." *Time*, XCVII (May 17, 1971), 94.

Hunt, Leigh. "Abou Ben Adhem." *Leigh Hunt as Poet and Essayist*. Edited by Charles Kent. London and New York: Frederick Warne & Co., Ltd., 1888.

Kazin, Alfred. "The Pilgrimage of Walker Percy." *Harper's Magazine*, CCXLII (June, 1971), 81–86.

Kennebeck, Edwin. "The Search." *Commonweal*, LXXIV (June 15, 1961), 260–62.

Kierkegaard, Søren. *Crisis in the Life of an Actress*. Translated by Stephen Crites. London: Collins, 1967.

_____. *For Self-Examination and Judge for Yourselves!* Translated by Walter Lowrie. Princeton: Princeton University Press, 1941.

_____. *Training in Christianity*. Translated by Walter Lowrie. Princeton: Princeton University Press, 1941.

McElroy, Davis Dunbar. *The Study of Literature, an Existential Appraisal*. New York: Philosophical Library, 1965.

McGuane, Thomas. "Love in the Ruins" (review). *New York Times Book Review*, May 23, 1971, sec. 7, pp. 7, 37.

Maluntschuk, Gregor. *Kierkegaard's Way to the Truth*. Translated by Mary Michelson. Minneapolis: Augsburg Publishing House, 1963.

Marcel, Gabriel. *Creative Fidelity*. Translated by Robert Rosthal. New York: Noonday Press, a division of Farrar, Straus and Giroux, 1964.

_____. *Man Against Mass Society*. Translated by G. S. Fraser. Chicago: Henry Regnery Company, 1952.

May, Rollo. *The Meaning of Anxiety*. New York: Ronald Press Company, 1950.

O'Connor, Flannery. *Mystery and Manners*. Edited by Sally and Robert Fitzgerald. New York: Farrar, Straus and Giroux, 1969.

Percy, Walker. "American War." *Commonweal*, LXV (March 29, 1957), 655–57.

_____. "Culture: The Antinomy of the Scientific Method." *New Scholasticism*, XXXII (October, 1958), 443–75.

_____. "Culture Critics." *Commonweal*, LXX (June 5, 1959), 247–50.

_____. "Decline of the Western." *Commonweal*, LXVIII (May 16, 1958), 181–83.

_____. "From Facts to Fiction." *Writer*, LXXX (October, 1967), 27–28, 46.

Percy, Walker. "How to Succeed in Business without Thinking about Money." *Commonweal*, LXXVII (February 22, 1963), 557–59.

_____. "The Loss of the Creature." *Forum*, II (1958), 6–14.

_____. "The Man on the Train." *Partisan Review*, XXIII (Fall, 1956), 478–94.

_____. "The Message in the Bottle." *Thought*, XXXIV (Fall, 1959), 405–33.

_____. "The Metaphor as Mistake." *Sewanee Review*, LXVI (Winter, 1958), 79–99.

_____. "Mississippi: The Fallen Paradise." *Harper's Magazine*, CCXXX (April, 1956), 166–72.

_____. "Modern Man on the Threshold." *America*, CV (August 12, 1961), 612.

_____. "New Orleans Mon Amour." *Harper's Magazine*, CCXXXVII (September, 1968), 80–82.

_____. "Red, White and Blue-Gray." *Commonweal*, LXXV (December 22, 1961), 337–39.

_____. "Semiotic and a Theory of Knowledge." *Modern Schoolman*, XXXIV (May, 1957), 225–46.

_____. "Seven Laymen Discuss Morality." *America*, CIV (October 1, 1960), 12–13.

_____. "Southern Moderate." *Commonweal*, LXVII (December 13, 1957), 279–82.

_____. "Southern View." *America*, XCVII (July 20, 1957), 428–29.

_____. "Stoicism in the South." *Commonweal*, LXIV (July 6, 1956), 342–44.

_____. "Symbol, Consciousness, and Intersubjectivity." *Journal of Philosophy*, LV (July 17, 1958), 631–41.

174

_____. "Symbol as Need." *Thought*, XXIX (Autumn, 1954), 381–90.

_____. "Truth or Pavlov's Dogs?" *America*, XCVII (June 8, 1957), 306–7.

_____. "Virtues and Vices in the Southern Literary Renaissance." *Commonweal*, LXXVI (May 11, 1962), 181–82.

_____. *Lost in The Cosmos: The Last Self-Help Book*. New York: Farrar, Straus and Giroux, 1983.

Ricoeur, Paul. *Freedom and Nature: The Voluntary and the Involuntary*. Translated by Erazim V. Kohák. Evanston: Northwestern University Press, 1966.

Rougemont, Denis de. *Dramatic Personages*. Translated by Richard Howard. New York, Chicago, San Francisco: Holt, Rinehart and Winston, 1964.

Sheed, Wilfrid. "The Good Word: Walker Percy Redivivus." *New York Times Book Review*, July 4, 1971, sec. 7, p. 2.

_____. "Ravening Particles of Anxiety," *Critic*, XXV (October–November, 1966), 92–93.

Swenson, David F. *Kierkegaardian Philosophy in the Faith of a Scholar*. Philadelphia: Westminister Press, 1949.

Tanner, Tony. *The Reign of Wonder*. Cambridge: University Press, 1965.

Thale, Mary. "The Moviegoer of the 1950's." *Twentieth Century Literature*, XIV (July, 1968), 84–89.

Thomte, Reidar. *Kierkegaard's Philosophy of Religion*. Princeton: Princeton University Press, 1948.

Whitehead, Alfred North. *Science and the Modern World*. New York: Free Press, 1925.

Wild, John. "Kierkegaard and Contemporary Existentialist Philosophy." *A Kierkegaard Critique*. Edited by Howard A. Johnson and Niels Thulstrup. New York: Harper and Brothers Publishers, 1962.

Wilkie, Brian. "The Last Gentleman" (review). *Commonweal*, LXXXIV (August, 19, 1966), 537–39.